SOS
SICK OF SEX

ROBYN McKELVY

S.O.S. — SICK OF SEX
Copyright © 2012 by Robyn McKelvy

PCG Legacy, a division of Pilot Communciations Group, Inc.
317 Appaloosa Trail Waco, TX 76712

Scripture quotations are from The Holy Bible, English Standard Version® (ESV®), copyright © 2001 by Crossway, a publishing ministry of Good News Publishers. Used by permission. All rights reserved.

ISBN: 978-1-936417-47-6

Printed in the United States of America

www.robynmckelvy.com

DEDICATION

For Ray—for making me believe I could.

Raychel, RayJ., Ross, Ryan, ReNay, Raegan, Ravin, Rhesa and Ryland and Sadie—for picking up the slack at home.

Mom—for making reading and writing a priority in our home.

Daddy—thanks for everything.

Chantele' and Stephanie—for telling me I needed to.

Mike, Cheri, John and Ethel—for my quiet rooms.

Dan and Candy—for pushing me.

Liz—for drawing it out for me.

Chris and Angie—for reading and babysitting for me.

Alice, Debra and Alyssa—for making me look good and sound smart.

God—for giving me the ability. Your strength is perfect. You are my All in All.

CONTENTS

INTRODUCTION

My husband Ray and I were leading a marriage conference at our church and we wanted our members to hear some of the topics from the FamilyLife "Weekend to Remember" conferences that we teach. With permission from FamilyLife, we presented the material that we witnessed was changing marriages around the world at every conference. One portion of the conference was on the differences in how men and women view sex. Both Ray and I shared general and personal differences. As I presented my differences to the women in the room, I said, "Come on, ladies. We want sex, too!" Everyone in the room laughed.

A couple of weeks later, one of the ladies at the church conference invited me to lunch. We had a nice meal and mostly talked about church issues. We had to pick up our children from school, so we rushed out the door of the café saying our goodbyes. As we arrived at our cars, she said, "I just want to know what you meant by

"We want sex, too...I don't want sex." Needless to say, we were both late picking up our kids! (I must add that this woman is not married to some slouch of a man with a beer belly who scratches himself all the time. Her husband is handsome and loves the Lord.)

Later that same evening, a young married couple dropped by our house, and I mentioned my lunch conversation. With the guys and kids out of the room, I shared with the wife how this lady was feeling about my response to sex. Then this young woman, who was also at the conference, asked, "You don't really like sex, do you?" I was floored.

Was I odd? Was sex something to tire of?

You might believe that I, of all people, would be one who would have a genuine complaint with sex; it has produced 15 pregnancies in my body. I have nine children and a very busy husband who all require my care from the moment I wake until my head hits the pillow. I have also struggled with male authority since I was a young girl. I am sure there are few women who would fault me if I were a little sick of sex. But I am not! I still find it a privilege to be intimate with Ray.

I believe a negative attitude about sex wages war against Christian marriages. It is a means of dividing couples in the most intimate way possible and is a quiet but deadly attack on Christian marriages. Any woman who has intimacy issues with her husband must know that it is an attack on her most precious earthly relationship. And Satan attacks this private area because he knows it is

7

such a delicate subject matter—we won't openly talk about it.

Satan tries to keep you bound in chains when it comes to secrets about your spouse and about your past. These chains have you stuck in bondage, sexually, and cause feelings of hopelessness. These chains also keep you from moving forward toward authentic intimacy.

The sexual abuse my husband experienced as a child was one of our chains. In trying to get me to understand how all the secrets trapped him, he wrote this poem:

The Secret

The secret is a shell that keeps my heart enclosed.
The secret is a shell that fears to be exposed.
The secret is a shell protecting me from pain.
The secret is a shell masking all the guilt and shame.
The secret is a shell that makes me feel alone.
The secret is a shell saying, "You can make it on your own."
The secret is a shell where I go and hide.
The secret is a shell in no one I can confide.
The secret is a shell that must be broken.
The secret is a shell; truth must be spoken.
The secret is a shell I'm planting in the ground.
The secret is a shell with life inside that's bound.
The secret is a shell; it's beginning to crack open.
The secret is a shell; my pride is being broken.
The secret is a shell that's rooted in a lie.
The secret is a shell when exposed to the truth will die.

The secret is a shell I'm finally letting out.
The secret is a shell no more hiding I can shout!

To be sick of sex is a cry for help; you desire to let the secret out and hide no more. By admitting that you are sick of sex, you have admitted at least one thing—you have signed an S.O.S. declaration—not "Sick of Sex," but *Save Our Ship*. Your relation*ship* is imperceptibly sinking, and the hole in the crucial portion of the ship, beneath the water, may seem too big to patch. But you have to know that unattended holes will eventually cause the entire ship to sink and cause injury or death to all those on board.

You've probably attempted to repair the hole by the use of a band-aid approach; you've decided it's easier to have a little interlude with him once a week or every ten days, so he will leave you alone the other 335 days a year. Yet, if you are a married couple committed to being obedient to God, you should often desire to be with one another in an intimate way. Both of you should desire to be intimate—not just him.

If you do not desire sexual intimacy with your husband, you are sailing on a ship that is destined to sink. This does not necessarily mean divorce, but it does mean existing in a dying marriage. A marriage that thrives requires above-average intimacy.

You must know that a sexual relationship is absolutely necessary and is a vital component of a healthy marriage. It is one that is full of life, and that life is granted

9

when both you and your spouse are free of the "secrets" in any area of marriage. This vitality is experienced the more we are freed from the secrets that rob our mental health.

Think about your sexual intimacy as a terminal illness for just a moment. What if every doctor, friend, and family member, alike, gave you no chance of recovery? But then, one physician gave you hope for a complete recovery and cure for any future outbreaks. You would hold onto that physician's diagnosis and look to him with trust and hope. In the same way, God, our Great Physician, can transform your sexual issues and aid you on to a healthy sexual relationship with your husband.

If this hits a little too close to home, do not despair! Although being sick of sex is a terminal illness to your marriage, there is hope. There is an antidote. I know that the truths in this book will bring healing, and the new signal you send will not be S.O.S.—Sick of Sex, but Super, Often Sex.

Every chapter written here is some form of S.O.S. cry. When you cry S.O.S. to the One who can save you, you must be ready to let go of what you are trusting in now. Then you can hold on to the true Lifesaver with both hands. You will be able to cling to the hope that Christ has to offer.

One of the beautiful things about sending out an S.O.S. signal is that you are requesting help. I pray this book will give you the hope you absolutely need to rehabilitate your sexual relationship with your husband. If the things herein are applied and taken to heart, it will give you a new and positive attitude about your sexual intimacy. Accept this prescription for a permanent recovery and apply all that the Great Physician prescribes.

Even now, do you believe that your Heavenly Father is capable of answering your prayer, healing your wounds, and creating an intimacy that you have only imagined?

Here's how you get there...

S.O.S.

SISTER, OH SISTER

A letter to all of you…

To all the ladies reading this book, I pray that this is a book that begins a path of freedom for all of us. For those of us that are living in sexual freedom, be thankful to God. The more I am given opportunity to speak about issues of intimacy, I am finding that there are so many women who are not experiencing freedom in intimacy because of sexual abuse perpetrated against them. I weep with you. I hate the evil that is tied to sexual intimacy. It is, in my opinion, one of the deepest and darkest evils there is.

There are many women who will try to read this book and it may bring to the surface the wounds of the abuse that happened or is happening. One friend told me she had to '…close the book. It made me so mad.' Another told me this book would not be for her; she thought her abuse was too great. I agree, maybe this is not the book for everyone, but there is truth in this book. If you are a woman that has experienced the pain associated with abuse, I encourage you to begin with the truth in the following chapters:

> 1) Search Out Sanctuaries—God is walking with you and wants you to be made whole. Even in this area. He is available. His Word is truth. He will never leave you. He loves you.
>
> 2) Soul Out Sister—God is so good to us. He has not left us to walk our life alone. We need to be passionate about finding genuine Godly women who are available to walk alongside us. Where are these women, you may ask? If you can't even think of one you know, ask God to reveal them to you. Seek a pen pal (we don't do that anymore, but boy do we need it again), there are e-mentoring sites that will set you up with a mentor online. Women are available and we don't want to allow the enemy any room to develop another lie that they are not there.
>
> 3) Shattering Old Systems—As you walk your path towards recovery. Stamp out all the lies with truth. It will set you free.

Continue to seek the truth. Never allow yourself to believe that your case is a hopeless cause. As long as God is in charge, there is hope…and He is in charge, FOREV-ER.

My prayer for you:

The Lord bless you and keep you; the Lord make his face to shine upon you and be gracious to you; the Lord lift up his countenance upon you and give you peace.[1]

— Robyn

[1] *The Holy Bible: English standard version.* 2001 (Nu 6:24-26). Wheaton: Standard Bible Society.

S.O.S. — CHAPTER #1

SHARE OUR STORIES: OLIVIA

"I'm certain that most couples expect to find intimacy in marriage, but it somehow eludes them." — Dr. James Dobson

I was born into a middle-class family. My father was a hard-working man, which allowed my mother to stay at home. I grew up with four sisters and one brother.

I never had a relationship with my father. I don't ever remember him telling me that he loved me. My parents were devoted Christians so we attended church at every opportunity. But there seemed to be no fun in our family. It was always about going to church or doing work. Love to me meant only the provision of food, clothing, or shelter. Affection was never shown in my family. I don't remember it between my parents or shown to us as children. Many people say, "You can't miss what you never had," but is that really true?

When I was 14, my father was killed in a work accident. Even with no affection shown to me, I felt like my protector was gone and I began looking to older men. I wanted men who would dominate, take charge, and put me in my place just like my dad put my mother in her place all those years. That is what a "normal" relationship looked like to me.

In high school, I took an interest in this street-smart guy who had a nice car. Because of my sheltered home, I was a very "good" girl. I did what I was told, mostly, and didn't create much need for discipline from my newly widowed mom. I had a boyfriend, but it was a pretty innocent relationship. Yet, this other guy was intriguing to me.

I felt that losing my dad took part of my childhood away so I began looking for something and not even knowing what to look for. I had little confidence and very poor self-esteem. Because of this hard period of my life, I began the cycle of always pleasing people.

The nice car pulled up in my driveway to collect me for our date. We rode out to his farm that day, and I remember going into the house but cannot recall how we entered the bedroom where he forcefully tied me to the bed and raped me. Confusion and a deep sense of feeling "bad" filled me as he drove me back to my home. I just had no idea what to do. I didn't even tell my family or call the police until the next day.

The rape changed me completely. I was not a virgin anymore. All the "good" girls in our church had not lost their virginity. I remember specifically saying to myself,

"There is nothing to save for marriage now." So I began having sex with my boyfriend.

Several of the men I dated later on were 10 to 15 years my senior. I was still looking for the love of my father. There was such a deep wound there. Because the value of a "relationship" was never verbalized in my family, I grew up thinking affection was optional. I began using sex, not for affection, but to keep men.

Then I met my husband. He is a Christian man but we never really talked about sexual intimacy before marriage; we just had sex. I saw him as different because he isn't the domineering type. He is very affectionate and considerate. Now after years of being married, things have changed, sexually. I am secure in my marriage so I see sex as optional. I don't want it and I don't have a need for it.

My husband, in his frustration, one day said to me, "You wanted it when we were dating." In turn, out of my own frustration, I told him, "I never wanted it then. I just kept doing 'it' to keep you."

I am not interested in sex, whatsoever, anymore. But I love my husband and I know my attitude must change. I know I have a need for counseling but time, finances, and lack of priority keep me from seeking it even though, at one time, my husband wanted a divorce.

To see me, you would never realize the distress I am in when it comes to intimate things. I function well on my job, I have taken care of my children well, and I'm at every soccer game. I am still an active churchgoer. I still

17

hear plenty of scripture and know that it is true. I desire to live a Christian life and often seek others for counsel on how to do that. But I walk around daily and feel like my heart is broken and all my thoughts of sex remain bad.

Growing up, I heard one scripture that is still so real to me: "But if you will not do so, behold, you have sinned against the Lord, and be sure your sin will find you out" (Numbers 32:23). My sin had found me out and still plagues my thoughts every day. The rape was devastating to me. Though I realize my rape was not my fault, my entire life was changed that day. I still have trouble forgiving the sins I committed against myself and I wish I had never voluntarily had sex before marriage.

***

My girlfriend, Olivia, made choices as a result of her rape that cast her into a spiral of false sexual intimacy. This false sexual intimacy has caused her to become sick of sex. Olivia is still bound by this conclusion today, and feels like there is no hope for her in this area. She has tried to change how she feels many times but believes, deep down, that things will never change. Olivia said to me, "You know how to work, you know how to take your kids to church, but ultimately, you don't know how to love your husband and your kids. You love them the best you know how, but the cycle continues."

She's right. The cycle must stop but you don't have to fight it alone.

"God is our refuge and strength, a very present help in trouble. Therefore we will not fear though the earth gives way, Though the mountains be moved into the heart of the sea, Though its waters roar and foam, though the mountains tremble at its swelling. Selah

There is a river whose streams make glad the city of God, The holy habitation of the Most High. God is in the midst of her; she shall not be moved; God will help her when morning dawns. The nations rage, the kingdoms totter; he utters his voice, the earth melts. The Lord of hosts is with us; the God of Jacob is our fortress. Selah

Come; behold the works of the Lord, How he has brought desolations on the earth. He makes wars cease to the end of the earth' He breaks the bow and shatters the spear; he burns the chariots with fire. "Be still, and know that I am God. I will be exalted among the nations; I will be exalted in the earth!" The Lord of hosts is with us; the God of Jacob is our fortress. Selah
— (Psalms 46:1-11)

For my friend, Olivia, and everyone else who believes they are stuck with this curse, God will be exalted in the earth. He is here to take back captives in every area. Our sovereign God was not asleep when the bad things happened to good people. He knows that evil will try to take away a life of freedom from all who believe. But He has a message for you, His child:

> No, in all these things we are more than con-
> querors through him who loved us. For I am
> sure that neither death nor life, nor angels
> nor rulers, nor things present nor things to
> come, nor powers, nor height, nor depth, nor
> anything else in all creation, will be able to
> separate us from the love of God in Christ
> Jesus our Lord. — (Romans 8:37-38)

S.O.S. JOURVOTIONAL

The following is your jourvotional for this chapter and every chapter will have a similar section for you to record your thoughts as you ponder important questions about that chapter's topic. I believe every person has a unique story and every book should have a reason to be read. Now it's your turn to write the story of your own intimacy. Journal your thoughts and feelings so you can remember today, look back later, and see how far God has brought you.

Answer the following questions, not just to gain more insight into the chapter you just read, but also to gain more insight into your personal road towards intimacy. Some of the questions will ask you about your experiences and some questions will allow you to devote some time in the truth of God's Word. Answer these as accurately as possible, knowing that God loves you and He will never leave you or forsake you on your journey.

Remember: To have devotions is to spend time with God, in His Word, see God's nature, and remember His purpose for your life.

JOURVOTIONAL

Share Our Stories: *Olivia*

1. Each one of us has a definition of love cast on us by our parents or other adults in our lives. To Olivia, her response to what she gathered from her parents is that love is "food, clothing, or shelter."

Think over your years growing up and use three words to describe what love means to you based on what was played out by your parents or those around you.

Growing up, love meant _____, _____, and _____

2. Describe your relationship with your father or other important men in your life when you were a young girl.

_____

_____

21

_____

_____

_____

_____

_____

3. How was affection shown in your family?

_____

_____

_____

_____

_____

4. Describe the affection between your parents.

_____

_____

_____

_____

_____

5. Describe the affection from your parents to you.

_____

_____

_____

_____

_____

_____

6. Growing up, did you feel like you had a protector and if so, who was it?

_____

_____

_____

_____

7. How was that protection displayed?

_____

_____

_____

_____

_____

_____

8. When is the first time you can remember desiring affection?

_____

_____

_____

9. Olivia's quests for love lead her to make choices she wanted to change. In your lifetime, has your own quest for love caused you to make choices you want to change?

_____

_____

_____

_____

_____

10. Read 1 Corinthians 13 and summarize what the Bible says love is.

_____

_____

_____

_____

_____

_____

_____

_____

_____

_____

_____

11. The Bible also says in 1 John 4:7-8, *"Beloved, let us love one another: for love is of God; and every one that loveth is begotten of God, and knoweth God. He that loveth not knoweth not God; for God is love."* What do the words "God is love" mean to you?

_____

_____

_____

_____

_____

_____

Praise the LORD! Oh give thanks to the LORD, for HE is good, for his steadfast love endures forever! — (Psalms 106:1)

S.O.S. — CHAPTER #2

SENDING OUT SIGNALS

....for man looks on the outward appearance, but the LORD looks on the heart. — (1 Samuel 16:7)

If you picked up this book out of your personal suffering, then you are one of millions of women who are sick of sex. Too many women are walking around with smiles on their faces, knowing that the most intimate expression of love in their relationship has one major flaw: You could live without sex.

When we have an area in our lives that constantly produces stress or strain, it shows. Even though the area is masked, we cannot hide the distress. Anyone in distress sends out distress signals and distress changes you. It causes you to lose out on your free spirit because you are hiding or masking your pain. This change, because of your distress, will cause you to become someone you are not and everyone in your world can tell something is bothering you. No matter how well you have learned to live with it, get through your day, and tolerate your stressed areas, those who know you best will know something is wrong.

Your Husband Knows

Do you give in to your husband when he desires intimacy but feel that if you didn't have to have sex in marriage, your marriage would be perfect? Not unlike cancer, "symptoms" of an ailing relationship may only appear occasionally, like in the privacy of your bedroom. You will seek help only when the symptoms are too damaging to ignore.

We don't need to wait long to hear jokes about men always wanting sex and women always having headaches. It makes you believe this is the norm; women are not supposed to enjoy sex. You may even feel like this is an area where it probably won't get better, but at least you're "normal." *After all, this area of the marriage is primarily for the enjoyment of our husbands.* But that's where the problems begin. Any area in your marriage where you and your husband are not striving to become one causes division and begins the process of isolating you from him.

Division causes distress because husband and wife are designed to be "one flesh" (Genesis 2:24). This division is evident to both wife and husband. It even spills over to the kids and others who are close to you.

When there are distress signals, you can be sure that your husband senses them. You may be the best actress in the world and think that he doesn't have a clue that you don't enjoy sex, but he knows something is wrong, even if he can't put his finger on it. He might not even have the wisdom to correlate that your distress has to do with sex but he knows that there is something that is not as free with you as it once might have been.

In the book of Esther, Esther is told by her uncle Mordecai that it is the intent of the Kings' right-hand man, Haman, to destroy the Jews. Esther, as Queen, has never disclosed to the King or anyone that she is Jewish. But when Mordecai reveals to Esther the plot to destroy their people, she is concerned that she could possibly perish if she enters the sight of the king unrequested.

Mordecai reminds her that she will perish, either way. Esther decides to go, unrequested, to see the king and says, "If I perish, I perish." Esther realizes to do nothing is to perish and to do something may mean she will perish, but she must do something. There comes a time in every relationship where there is an area where you must fight until the death. Sexual intimacy with your husband is one area where you must be willing to die fighting for it to become a positive, enjoyable experience.

Admittedly, there may be many valid reasons for your distress in the sexual area. Your husband many not be sensitive to your needs or his approach to sex might be more uninhibited than you are comfortable with. But whether you believe it or not, your husband wants sex to be just as enjoyable to you as it is to him. He wants you to be a willing participant and fulfilled every time you have sex with him. Every husband wants his wife to initiate sexual intimacy with him. *He wants you to want him!*

To dread, avoid, or hate this intimate time with your husband is not just your issue. It is not just his issue, either. It is both of yours and will not be resolved unless both of you are willing to address the distress and expose the lies. Any issue that affects one of you affects both of you. And your intimacy or lack thereof, is one BIG issue.

I enjoy the re-runs of the TV series *Everybody Loves Raymond.* In one episode, Raymond was desperately approaching his wife, Debra, to have sex with him that night. Debra did the whole "I'm tired" routine but promised to have sex with him the next day. Raymond got out

29

a piece of paper and wrote: "I, Debra, agree to have sex with Raymond tomorrow on May 23, of this year...." He then tapped Debra on the back and asked her to sign the paper.

How would we feel if the preacher stood before us on our wedding day with these inspiring words: "I, (your name), take thee, (your husband's name), for my lawfully wedded husband. For better, for worse, for richer, for poorer, in sickness and in health. To love, honor and cherish; keeping only unto him to regularly have sex with him, until death do we part." We would be flabbergasted! Sex is a given. No one should have to make us promise. No one should have to dread sex. No one should have to require sex, and, definitely, no one should have to beg for sex. As Paul counsels, "The wife's body does not belong to her alone but also to her husband. In the same way, the husband's body does not belong to him alone but also to his wife. Do not deprive each other except by mutual consent and for a time, so that you may devote yourselves to prayer" (1 Corinthians 7:4-5).

The enemy works to ensure we deprive each other of more than prayer. If there was that much praying going on, we would see so many more healthy relationships and a whole lot less distress. Sadly, our children, our husbands, our best friends, our co-workers, and our God are seeing a lot of distressed marriages and not as many healthy, intimate relationships.

Intimacy is healthy and good. It is biblical and it is designed by God. God wants your husband to want you, and for you to desire your husband! Even in a woman's physical makeup, she alone is given a sexual organ, the clitoris, that's *only* purpose is sexual pleasure.

God also gave us the Song of Solomon to know that sex is for mutual pleasure. Here, God allows us to see into the soul of a woman who genuinely longs for her husband. God reveals that the husband not only has the right to admire his wife's body, but the wife should also admire her husband's body. God knew we would have to see it in writing or we just wouldn't believe it!

If you are sick of sex, you certainly do not want to take the time to admire your husband's body. The last thing on earth that you want is your husband to have a huge ego about his body. Then, you give him permission to turn his attention to your body. And we all know that when he focuses on your body, the very thing that you don't want, he has to have.

The Shulamite woman, the beloved woman of the Song of Solomon, has instead embraced her husband in every way. She describes Solomon's body using things that have special meaning to her. When is the last time you admired your husband's body and used something that was special to you to describe him? And I don't mean, "Your belly is like a big bowl of ice cream. And I mean a big, big bowl!" But your husband would love for you to use this illustration if you followed it with, "And, Sweetie, I can't wait to dig in!"

Now, to some of you, ice cream all over his body sounds like another mess to clean up, and you already

31

have enough housework. As much as we may laugh about this, the stark reality is that our husbands are affected, deeply and holistically, by our lack of desire for and rejection of him in the most intimate of moments, because that's what our apathy towards sex truly is.

For many men, their egos are tied to their sexual relationship, so if your husband does know that you are sick of sex, it becomes a huge strike against his manhood. Every time you reject your husband sexually, you hit him at the core of his masculinity.

Our husbands are affected, deeply and holistically, by our lack of desire for and rejection of him in the most intimate of moments.

This rejection cripples your husband in other areas of life. Do you wonder why he is passive or complacent? He has been rejected in his most vulnerable area.

In the privacy of your bedroom, your husband should be able to be the boy inside. He should be able to be full of fun, laughter, and anticipation. He should be able to be his rambunctious self. His intimacy with you should allow him the freedom to be full of the youthful energy that, in a perfect world, would have been uninhibited.

His intimacy with you, sexually and personally, should give him confidence to take on the world.

Your Children Know

When there are distress signals, your children know

32

it. Children adapt quickly and learn that these signals are considered "normal" and they will grow up and exhibit the same behavior.

By our actions, we leave our children a marital legacy. Think about it. We spend too much time making sure that we leave our children a solid legacy in every other area. We want to make sure that their financial legacy is set. We absolutely want to make sure that they pick the right spouse so that their family's heritage and happiness is set. But, our children will desire marriage based on how they view your marriage. In fact, without a dogged determination not to, they may carry on your distress signals—tension, disconnect, sharp or selfish responses, and a lack of honesty—right into their own bedrooms. Your marriage, good or bad, will lay the foundation for the establishment of your children's marriages.

Through modeling, parents either leave a bitter or sweet taste in the mouths of their children, concerning marriage. And if the most intimate part of your marital relationship is strained, you can guarantee that you will leave a negative view of marriage for your children. The question is, "How do you want your children to view sexual intimacy in marriage?"

Kids need to see a healthy marital relationship lived out before them, daily, by their mother and father. Whether you say one word or not to them about any damaged area of your marriage, your children will know the climate of your intimacy. Even if you've avoided verbally communicating your destructive mentality regarding your sexual intimacy, you've fooled yourself into believing that you can keep this private tension in the bedroom. Once again, sex is an indicator of the rest of your relationship. Children can sense and feel when it is not as healthy as God intended. And your children, like you, will try to make up for the lack of healthy intimacy through their performance or by trying to fix the relationship.

When intimacy is strained between you and your husband, your children will know and use it to their advantage. It is easier for children to pit parent against parent when you are struggling intimately. *Strained intimacy cultivates division and distress.* (Satan uses even this to get you to focus on what's going on with the kids instead of dealing with your own intimacy issues.)

Some children will try to perform better at school, sports, or other activities to take the focus off whatever is ailing their parents and place it on themselves. And some children will become destructive to themselves because of strained parental intimacy. Their security is established in the loving relationship of their parents to each other. It gives them a sense of safety. Take away a child's safety net and they do whatever is necessary to try to feel safe again (good or bad).

By continuing to let this area remain in distress, you are creating a family epidemic. When your children marry, they will tolerate mediocrity in their own most intimate relationship. Think about what your son will anticipate in regards to intimacy with his own wife. How will your daughter respond to her knight in shining armor when he approaches her for intimacy?

As long as you allow your marriage to remain in sexual distress, you are setting a legacy where this distress will be a way of life, especially for your children. The world already has your children by two feet, pulling them down to its view of sex. We must pull our children up and give them the right view of intimacy. This is done in our homes as we learn and apply a godly view of sexual intimacy.

Whether we want to admit it or not, most of our marriages look like our parents' marriages. We have a tendency to clean the kitchen like our mothers and mow the lawn in the same pattern that our fathers did. Likewise, our parents were our teachers in the area of marital relationships. If your mother and father responded to each other with little or no affection, your natural tendency is to respond to your husband in the same way. It is very difficult to change something that you have seen all your life. After all, we not only have to identify that the behavior is wrong (and not normal), but we also have to find and apply the right biblical behavior to an incorrect view of sexual intimacy. This will be a *difficult* and not easily accomplished task, but it's *not* an impossible one.

We must passionately pursue all that God would have our relationship to be (He knows how He designed relationships to work best for our holiness). But we must remember John 10:10: "The thief comes only to steal and kill and destroy. I came that they may have life and have it abundantly." So many of us have simply settled and are

35

stuck in a sexual rut, even in a place of fear, in this sexual experience. Someone once said, "Satan does everything he can to get us into bed before we are married and everything to keep us out of bed when we get married."

Our children need to anticipate sexual intimacy in their own marriages because of the solid foundation we have laid out for them. And if we haven't laid it for them, we must be willing to allow our children to see us, with passion, seek to fight to attain it.

Your Best Friend Knows

When distress is looming in your marital relationship, your best friend knows it. For those of us who will talk about sex, we still don't want too much of the focus of this area to be on us. We don't allow our friends to elaborate, get serious, or get intimate about this area when it comes to our lives. We keep sexual intimacy conversations, even with our friends, superficial. It's easy to put on a face and not allow anyone to know that there is a strain in this intimate area of our "perfect" lives. There are even those who may not keep it superficial but we try to pretend that this area isn't that important anyways, "It's no big deal."

The horrific problem here is that you are probably friends with other couples who could give you a lift up when you are down. These friends would be able to offer you truth when you can't see the truth for yourself but you're afraid to be open and honest with them. And oftentimes, we are so busy "protecting our privacy" that we don't even have intimate friends anymore. Satan has not only divided your most intimate relationship, he is dividing couples from truly sharing intimately, so we can build up one another's marriages. We must get to the place where we trust our friends.

Most of us, in high school, had at least one friend we would tell anything to. We were not afraid she would ever leak our confidence. (And that was probably before most of us were Christians). Now we not only have friends who will pray with us, but they will live with us—eternally. We have to learn to open up and trust others again. This is an urgent, unmet need in our marriages and we will elaborate more on this need in the Sold Out Sister chapter of this book.

Your Co-workers Know

Our distress is also displayed to a world wanting to know the truth about marriage. The world wants to see authentic love displayed between a husband and wife. People in your workplace want to experience the fruit of authentic love and are begging to see a true picture of this. Those in your sphere of influence have seen too many fake imitations, and they are crying out for a glimpse of what the real thing looks like. We, as Christians, are called to be salt and light to the world. Matthew 5:13-16 says, "You are the salt of the earth, but if salt has lost its taste, how shall its saltiness be restored? It is no longer good for anything except to be thrown out

37

and trampled under people's feet. You are the light of the world. A city set on a hill cannot be hidden. Nor do people light a lamp and put it under a basket, but on a stand, and it gives light to all in the house. In the same way, let your light shine before others, so that they may see your good works and give glory to your Father who is in Heaven."

If the truth be known, it is no longer just the world that desires to see models of a good marriage. Christians are secretly desiring it and waiting to see who will lead them to fulfillment. Which of us Christians will take the lead? Those who do not know Christ are waiting for authentic people to display marriages of true love—not riding-off-into-the-sunset-love, but marriages that go the distance, showing loving-when-loving-is-really-difficult love.

It is a shame that even Christian marriages are lacking in this area that God created for our enjoyment. God wants sex to be fun, exciting, passionate, and intense. God tells us in His Word to rejoice. He wants us to feel "great delight" in things, just as He tells us in Philippians 4:4 to "Rejoice in the Lord always; and again I will say, Rejoice." The same "great delight" that we find in God, He wants us to find in one another. Proverbs 5:18-20 says, "Let your fountain be blessed, and rejoice in the wife of your youth, a lovely deer, a graceful doe. Let her breasts fill you at all times with delight; be intoxicated always in her love." These verses epitomize the fun, excitement, passion, and intensity God longs to bring to our marriages through sexual intimacy.

Without God's perspective about your sexual relationship in marriage, your whole marriage is missing out on all that He has planned for it to be. Wouldn't you want your marriage to be so great that it would bring glory to God in such a way that others would feel like they are missing out if they don't get themselves some of what you have? In essence, by seeing your marriage, people in this world could desire a godly marriage of their own. Children would see godly families and desire them, and the face of our culture would be forever changed.

God, Our Father, Knows

When this distress signal flashes, the most intimate being in our life knows—God, Himself. We often allow Him to only have access to some areas of our lives. We treat God as if to say, "As long as I don't mention this 'little' area in prayer to you, then I don't have to deal with this area. After all, Lord, I spend time with you every day. Isn't that enough? I am not perfect and you know my imperfections." But deep inside we are in turmoil because we know we cannot hide the truth from God. We may be able to wear a mask with everyone else, but God sees behind the mask.

We have to change the way we look at sex. The only way to do that is to acknowledge that we are also sending distress signals to God. Even though we know that we serve a miracle-working God, we do not see that this situation is volatile enough to demand a miracle. Many times, because we "think" this is a hidden area, or even believe it isn't so necessary, we may not believe or even care to see God change our mindset about sex. We may even think that there are so many things we have placed before the throne of grace that this one issue will either work itself out in time or we can handle it on our own.

We have to face the fact that if our sexual intimacy with our husbands is hindered in any way, it can be an indication that our relationship with God is also hindered. Intimacy hindered often makes us attempt to hide who we are and how we feel with God, our Heavenly Father. As long as we pretend, place it on the back burner, or overlook it and go on as though this personal sexual relationship with our husband is no big deal, we disallow God full access to our relationship so He can bring it to His perfection. We also disallow God full access to work on our heart and mind to change our perception of intimacy. We must surrender it all to God. God hears and sees the distress signals but is waiting for an opportunity to do His perfect work.

In Matthew 14:28-31, Peter walks on water at the Lord's command: "And Peter answered him, 'Lord, if it is you, command me to come to you on the water.' He said, 'Come.' So Peter got out of the boat and walked on the water and came to Jesus. But when he saw the wind, he was afraid, and beginning to sink he cried out, 'Lord, save me.' Jesus immediately reached out his hand and took hold of him saying to him, 'O, you of little faith, why did you doubt?'"

This incident happened just a couple of hours after Peter witnessed Jesus breaking five loaves of bread and two fish to feed 5,000 people. And even at this point in the story, Peter had started to walk on water. He was on his way to Jesus. But outside influences, the high winds and waves, made him afraid and caused him to sink, not to mention, doubt.

At any given time, a number of outside influences are always attacking our marriages. When we began our marriage, we felt like we could make it through anything with this great man God had given us. Now we have let difficulties influence us and cause us to doubt that we can make it. More specifically, we doubt God is able to turn our sexual relationship around, even though we see miracles all around us and have witnessed them with our own eyes. We don't see our distress in this sexual area as what it really is—desperate.

Peter cried out to the Lord, out of desperation, and Jesus was immediately there. God is right there for you, too. He has already seen and felt the distress signals you are sending, and He has the answer. He can perform this miracle. You just have to trust. Our God is the same yesterday, today, and forever. And God is more than capable of miraculously healing your sexuality and your sexual intimacy with your husband!

Have you cried out to the Lord out of desperation for His divine help in this area? And then once you cried out, have you allowed God to reach out His hand and take hold of you to steady your steps and take the doubt away?

God has chosen you for your husband. Your husband is unique, but God has uniquely equipped you to meet his needs. You are a mate "suitable for him" (Genesis 2:18) and "fashioned" for him (Genesis 2:22).

In 1 Corinthians 7:34 it says, "But the married woman is anxious about worldly things, how to please her husband." It is pointed out in this passage that as married women, our focus should also be on pleasing our husbands. Your husband is your priority. Just as you are his. This is not wrong; it is the truth.

To eliminate the distress signals in our marriages, we must truly desire to love our husbands as Christ has loved us. "This is how we know what love is: Jesus Christ laid down his life for us" (1 John 3:16). Are we willing, as Christ is, to lay down our lives for our husbands? The wonderful thing that God did for us even while we were still disobedient to Him and His Word was He sent Christ to die for us (Romans 5:8). Are we willing to lay down our right to get even with our husbands when we feel wronged? Are we willing to lay down our attitude of unforgiveness when he may not even know that he wounded us with his words...or even if he KNOWS he has wounded us with his words?

Are we willing to repay good for evil as the Bible tells us to do in Romans 12:21 when our own husbands may not be treating us the way we know he is supposed to treat us? Are we willing to allow the Lord to take vengeance when we want to so badly? In order to eliminate distress signals in your marriage, you must be willing to treat your husband the way Christ has treated you because this is how the Lord has shown His love to us (Romans 5:8) and we should, likewise, show love to our husbands. Love shown when one may not deserve it is unconditional and has no expectations of return. To remove distress signals from your intimacy with your husband, unconditional love must become the way you respond to him.

> *Create in me a clean heart, O God, And renew a right spirit within me.* — (Psalm 51:10)

JOURVOTIONAL

Sending Out Signals

1. Is sexual intimacy a stressed area for you? _____ For your husband? _____

2. Do you feel like the stress of your intimate relationship has changed your outlook on life's events? If so, how?

_____

_____

_____

3. If you answered "yes" to question 1, why do you think that the stress of sexual intimacy between you and your husband is present?

_____

_____

4. If you answered "no" to question 1, what are some things you are doing now to keep you and your husband from having stressed intimacy?

_____

_____

_____

5. Do you feel that you and your husband equally desire sexual intimacy? _____

6. What are some things you are doing to make sure that your intimacy continues to build for you both?

_____

_____

7. Do you believe that your husband "wants you to want him"? In what ways do you initiate intimacy with him?

_____

_____

_____

8. Describe your intimate relationship with your husband in one of these two phrases, "passive or complacent" or "passionate and confident." What are your reasons for your description of your intimacy?

_____

_____

_____

_____

_____

9. Do you feel you are leaving a healthy impression of intimacy to your children? Give examples why or why not.

_____

_____

_____

_____

10. What are some things you would change about your impression of intimacy before you were married?

_____

_____

_____

_____

_____

11. What are some things your children would say they would change about their impression of intimacy displayed by you when they are married?

_____

_____

_____

_____

_____

12. Who are your best friends? Your couple friends?

_____

_____

_____

_____

13. Are they aware of the condition of your intimacy (whether it is experiencing difficulty or moving towards oneness)?

_____

14. Is your personal picture of intimacy to those who don't have a Christian marriage one that shows the realness of a growing intimacy? Or is it an imitation of love?

_____

_____

15. Sexual intimacy is very personal and private. Most often if there are difficult elements in our intimacy, we seldom talk about them. God truly knows what your struggles are. But is intimacy an area you are choosing not to address with Him? What are some of your most intimate areas that you have either "hidden" or haven't addressed with God?

_____

_____

_____

_____

God desires to show his power in every area including your sexual intimacy. Read these verses and know that God has done it and will do it again. He will create a clean heart for you and he will renew a right spirit within you.

> "But you, O God my Lord, deal on my behalf for your name's sake; because your steadfast love is good, deliver me! For I am poor and needy, and my heart is stricken within me. I am gone like a shadow at evening; I am shaken off like a locust. My knees are weak through fasting; my body has become gaunt, with no fat. I am an object of scorn to my accusers; when they see me, they wag their heads. Help me, O Lord my God!

Save me according to your steadfast love! Let them know that this is your hand; you, O Lord, have done it! Let them curse, but you will bless! They arise and are put to shame, but your servant will be glad!" — (Psalm 106:21-28)

Simple Ways to Begin Diminishing Distress Signals

1. Admit to God that you have distress in this area and continually pray for His wisdom on alleviating it.

2. Get 2 or 3 friends to pray with you and hold you accountable in keeping this desire to alleviate distress a priority.

S.O.S. — CHAPTER #3

SETTING OUR STAGE

"Many marriages would be better if the husband and the wife clearly understood that they are on the same side." — Zig Ziglar

Simply put, sex takes preparation. Our lives are filled with preparation for our families. We keep a clean house. We prepare meals that are close to nutritionally sound. We try to look nice when we go out. We clean our piles of laundry to make sure our family has clean clothes to put on. But in the area of sex, unlike all the other "obvious" responsibilities, we have decided to take little effort. We are so tired from meeting our family's other needs that we have forgotten to prepare for the needs of our intimacy.

There are chores that we don't like to do so we wait as long as possible to take care of them. Those of us who do not like to do the laundry are the ones who usually put it off until we are down to our last pair of undies and have no other choice. (We even bought a new package of underwear at Wal-mart to make that in-between time just a little bit longer).

I mean, really, who likes to wash dishes? So when the dishwasher is broken, we let the dishes pile up in the sink until we're really thirsty, but there are no clean glasses. Then, if there are no kids (or husband) around, we do the dishes out of necessity. We are parched, and that crusty glass with yesterday's dried chocolate milk just can't be rinsed out anymore.

Many of our chores like laundry and dishes aren't done in a timely manner because life has us so busy. Unfortunately, many of us have put sex in the "chores to put off until absolutely necessary" category.

But as we've seen in Song of Solomon, sex should be something anticipated with excitement by a couple, not something to put off for as long as possible. Too many of us women have forgotten to do one thing: Prepare for sex.

What's in Your Bedroom?

In order to prepare for intimacy and have a different attitude about it, your bedroom must be a safe haven. When you enter your bedroom, it must be an "ahhh" place. Sex is different for men and women. Generally, sex to him can be at any time, any place. But for most of us, it is all about the setting—an intimate location gives us permission for intimacy.

If, in your bedroom, you have a pile of clean laundry on the bed and give your husband the signal (or just bending over to move the clothes is signal enough for some of our husbands), then sex is on to him. That pile of laundry just became a new mattress pad or has a new home on the floor (in one sweep). Now, even though your husband is waiting on the bed with that "Honey, come on" look, you only see that pile of clothes lying all over the dusty, dirty floor, and the feeling is gone. Poof!

Your bedroom has to stay de-cluttered in order to have a place where sexual intimacy is a turn on for you. Having nine children, I know about the woes of laundry. Every day when we change into our pajamas, there are two new loads of laundry waiting for me. But for me to have the proper place to enhance intimacy with Ray, I can't let my bedroom become the temporary dwelling place for clean (or dirty) laundry. My bedroom must be a place to enhance intimacy. Anything that reminds you that there is someone other than you and your husband dwelling there is in the wrong place. Create an "ahhh" place and not a "catch-all" place.

When Raychel, our oldest, came home from the hospital, we placed her in a bassinet in our room. After 5 weeks, we were getting into the groove of this thing called parenting. I could lift Raychel out of the bassinet, feed her with my eyes closed, and put her back without losing much sleep. Then, my cute, little baby turned 6 weeks old, and Ray began moving all her stuff into her own room. Being a new mom, I felt like it was my place to have that little baby close so I could protect her. Ray didn't have the same maternal need that I had. (Every time the baby squirmed, he was awakened by either me or her). He wanted to protect our relationship and I reluctantly let him. I needed to let Ray preserve our "marriage bed."

The only signs of your children in your bedroom should be a few pictures of them or things made by them. Be careful, because too many of these could cause you to focus on the wrong person in your bedroom. There should be no other signs of your children in your bedroom. Your children (no matter how few or many) need to have their own space and must respect yours. Your bedroom is you and your husbands' haven and no one other than the two of you should dwell or keep their stuff there, ever!

In order to change your attitude of being sick of sex, you must de-clutter your bedroom. Remove all the things that do not belong there and don't let them creep back in.

To set your stage and keep it performance ready, there are some simple things that you can do so the show can go on. Make your bed every day! It doesn't have to be fancy like a showroom in a Bed & Bath magazine. It just needs to be made.

When you go to a hotel for a romantic weekend, how would you feel if you checked in only to find your bed unmade? You would immediately go back downstairs and demand a room with a made bed. (There must be some mistake!) But what if you went downstairs and the attendant behind the desk said to you, "We don't make beds here anymore because we've found that all our guests mess them up anyway. We make sure that you have clean sheets but to make sure our housekeepers are not mis-managing time, we've decided to omit the making of beds." You would stand there for a minute, then kindly or not so kindly, request to checkout. Well, every time you enter your bedroom with an unmade bed, you checkout. This unmade bed reminds you of all the stuff you still have yet to get done.

Another simple thing that you can do is keep your room picked up. To walk over piles of clothes, shoes, or whatever is on the floor will soon frustrate you. Frustration is one of the main reasons we remain in a sick of sex state. (To be sick of sex, your husband is not neces-sarily the source of your frustration).

But, there are cases when you are angry with your husband. You believe if he would pick up his stuff, then you would have a clean room. Here is where you have to remember why God created you. Your husband needs help. You are his helper, his personal assistant to be exact. *I know this sounds a little "old school" but keep reading.*

Some of our husbands are on the other end of the spectrum. They are such perfectionists that not one shoe in the room can be out of place. God made you right for him. You are his perfect fit. You are here to help him understand that one shoe out of place does not make the room any less attractive for you. You love him. You have the ability to make that man forget to wear his own shoes the next day!

In Genesis 2:18, God said, "It is not good that the man should be alone, I will make a helper fit for him."

God was concerned for this man He created and wanted to make sure he had all he needed for his life. That perfect provision was woman.

You are in the perfect position to teach him that as Solomon, the wisest of all men, says in Ecclesiastes 4:9, "Two are better off than one, because together they can work more effectively." Teach him, by how you respond to him, that you are his ally and not his enemy.

In order to set your stage, remember two people share this room, and it has to be conducive for both. When a couple is married and share a bedroom, both personalities should be reflected in that space. One of you may be neat and everything is hung up, orderly, in the closet. The other may be not as neat and throw his things on the floor. Reflect and respect his personality, too. Just get a cute basket where he can throw his things.

I make sure that my living room or entry way is always kept neat because I want the area where guests mostly enter to be presentable. I want our guests to have an impression that clean, neat living is important to me. It is a reflection of my entire home. If life was perfect, my entire home would look like the living room. But because of obligations going on inside and outside of the home, that is only a dream.

Let me suggest, though, that your bedroom be one of the rooms that takes priority on the cleaning list. Let the care of your bedroom be a reflection of how important your husband is to you. Also, be sure the lock on your door actually works. Don't let a broken doorlock keep you from getting in the mood!

Understanding "Have To" Versus "Get To"

There are many things in life we most definitely have to do. Our "have to" list is unending. We must put gas in the car for it to go any distance. Gasoline is a have to. We must buy groceries before we can prepare dinner. Grocery shopping is a have to. The needs for hydration, nutrition, exercise, and entertainment are have to's. Without all of these components, you will become dehydrated, malnourished, immobile, and crabby.

There is one problem with our have to's; we've gotten so used to having to we've forgotten the privileges that come with get to's. Sex is not a have to. Sex is a get to.

No other person in the universe has the right to be sexually involved with your spouse and no other person, other than your husband, has the right to be sexually involved with you.

When Ray's mom gave birth to him, she laid gentle kisses all over his body. This was a sign of her maternal love for him. As his mother, she got to bathe him, feed him, and raise him to maturity. As his wife, I get to lip-lock Ray as long as I want, kissing him with passion. I get to bathe with him if I choose, share food off his plate, drink out of his cup, and be with him until either he or I steps foot into eternity. These are get to's!

55

We should never mistake a "get to" for a "have to." We must remember the benefits of life God has bestowed upon us. God's benefits are the get to's. Psalm 103:2 says, "Bless the Lord, O my soul, and forget not all his benefits."

My single girlfriends are fun to be with, and we often stay up later than Ray when they come over to visit. At the end of our visit, I get to lie next to Ray, steal his warmth, and place my cold feet next to his warm body. This is a benefit I have that my single friends do not. I am sure they are grateful for the place that God has them in. For me, I am grateful for my human heating pad. We must begin to see our marriage and sexual intimacy with our mate as "get to's."

A "get to" is a privileged opportunity that you accept with pleasure. A "get to" has to be maintained as an honored benefit in order for it to remain a "get to" and not slip into "have to" status.

Have you ever taken a cold shower because the gas was off, and you had no idea where or when the money to turn it on was coming? Maybe it is not just a day of cold showers but months. You must realize that the warm shower you take on a daily basis (oftentimes more than once a day) is a "get to."

Shortly after moving from Kansas City to Dallas, I was in the hospital having our second son, Ross. We were broke and had little food in our home. We had no friends, family nearby, or church home, yet. Times were so tough. We would ask the nurses to bring any extra food trays to my hospital room. But, at home, Ray and our two other kids ate peanut butter and jelly, everyday. This was a have to; it was all that we had. Ray's mother arrived a few days later and asked Ray to stop at the grocery store on the way home from the airport. She wanted to prepare a special meal. She blessed us with mouth-watering steak, flakey biscuits, and the works. Oh, how we appreciated this Heaven-sent meal! This time in our lives helped us to understand and appreciate the things we take for granted and understand the true meaning of have to's versus get to's.

Eating something every day is a "get to." Eating something different everyday is a "get to." Having more than one meal everyday is a "get to" and having more than one item at those meals is a Get-to-Blessing.

Do you realize the privilege of accepting God's divine gift to you in the form of your husband? When God set order to this world, he knew that you would be married to your husband. He is not surprised that the two of you are married. But do you understand that your husband needs you to care for him?

He needs to be able to count on you, above all, to "have his back." Other men should desire to be so lucky as to be placed with such a woman as you. He gets to be married to you, and he knows that you will "do Him good and not evil all the days of your life" (Proverbs 31:14). He should always feel like being married to you is a Get-to-Blessing and not a "have to stay married, Lord, because I am a Christian, and I am stuck" curse.

Do you know that you will, one day, give an account of all the gifts that God has entrusted to you? Your husband is one of the most prominent gifts given to you by our Holy, All-knowing Father. Do you understand what it means when Proverbs 31 says, "He is known in the gates because of her"?

How is your husband known? Are people looking to him and pitying him because his home life is a "train wreck"? Or are others glad to visit your home because they can be themselves there, including your husband?

My oldest daughter, Raychel, came home after babysitting one day. She told me how thankful she was that I did not talk to her daddy like that mother talked to her husband. Raychel was embarrassed for that husband and ashamed of his wife. When this wife talked to her husband in front of Raychel, it was demanding and demeaning. I don't know what her frustrations were at that moment, but to a young single girl, it made her uncomfortable with the couple and she wanted to get out of there. We need to have reverence for our husbands, save any necessary correction for our private bedroom conversations, and remember there is someone always watching your marriage relationship. Our young people desire to see healthy, mutually fulfilling marriages.

Do you ever wonder why this new generation has decided to forego marriage and just live together? Marriage is no longer desirable to this generation. Marriage has become a "have to" to them. Sex is now totally accepted outside marriage. We have demonstrated this "have to" mentality to our kids and they don't see the awesome gift of marriage as a "get to."

Unfortunately, the world has decided they can't make a better relationship than what they see Christians trying to accomplish. They've decided to forget the part that is right in the sight of God. Satan lies to the world and tells them they have to have sex, and they get to get married. But in order for God to honor their relationship, they have to get married, and get to have sex.

We must recapture the beauty and desire of sex in marriage as something to be sought after. Every time you have sex in marriage it should be a "get to." Yet, so many of us feel this attitude can never be recaptured.

God has heard your distress signals, and He wants to give you healing in this area. He wants you to desire an intimate, unhindered relationship with Him and with your husband. He just needs you to see the situation as desperate enough to trust that He, and He alone, can fix it.

In Matthew 9:27-30, Jesus encounters two blind men: "And as Jesus passed on from there, two blind men followed him, crying aloud, 'Have mercy on us, Son of David.' When he entered the house, the blind men came to him, and Jesus said to them, 'Do you believe that I am able to do this?' They said to him, 'Yes, Lord.' Then touched their eyes, saying, 'According to your faith be it done to you.' And their eyes were opened."

Are your eyes open? How big is your faith? Do you believe that God is able to alleviate this distress and begin forming a healthy, restored intimacy in your relationship? Say, "Yes, Lord," and watch God open your relational eyes. If you continue to pretend your wounded relationship is okay, then you have signed a permission slip to propel your marriage—and influence the marriages of your children, your friends, and an on-looking world—into the murky depths of complacency.

Choose a marriage that's on fire and believe that God is able. Take His outstretched hand. Soon all who draw near to your marriage, that God has worked His miracles to create, will experience warmth in their hearts and a model to pattern their own lives after.

Change can happen. I suggest you begin with this short prayer:

> Dear Lord,
> I really need Your help! I am in a place where sex feels like a "have to," and I really would like to get to the place where I can view it as a "get to." I feel hopeless in this area. Would You please change my heart and my mindset, Lord? I don't want to affect my children and those around me negatively, in this most intimate area. I don't have the power to overcome this by myself. Please, change me. In Jesus' name, Amen.

JOURVOTIONAL

Setting Our Stage

1. Is your bedroom an "ahhh" place? Is it a haven for you and your husband? _____

2. What would make or does make your bedroom an intimate place for you?

_____

_____

_____

3. What are some of the things in your bedroom that do not belong to you or your husband?

_____

_____

_____

_____

4. Why are they there?

_____

_____

_____

5. Is your bedroom "performance" ready? _____

6. What are some of the special things (props, if you will) in your bedroom that say sexual intimacy is welcomed here? (Excluding the bed.)

_____

_____

_____

8. Is your bedroom high on the cleaning/keep neat priority list? ____

9. Do you view sex as a "have to" or a "get to"? Why?

_____

_____

_____

_____

_____

10. When your children observe your marriage and how you relate to and care for your husband, would it make them desire marriage or not want it for themselves?

_____

_____

_____

11. What are some of things about your marriage that you think are attractive to them?

_____

_____

_____

_____

12. What are some of things about your marriage that could be unattractive to them?

_____

_____

_____

_____

13. "For as he thinketh in his heart, so is he" (Proverbs 23:7). When you think about sex, what are your deepest, hidden thoughts about sexual intimacy?

_____

_____

_____

_____

_____

_____

14. Are these thoughts helping you or hindering you from setting a stage of intimacy that continues to move your relationship toward genuine godly intimacy?

_____

_____

_____

_____

Simple Ways to Begin to Set Your Stage

1. Make your bed and add one cute girly pillow.

2. Keep linen spray close by and freshen your pillows with it on occasion.

3. Keep a nice smelling candle in your room and light it, ever-so-often, for a special boost to your bedroom's air.

4. Use a great smelling lotion after your shower at night.

5. Memorize Proverbs 23:7.

S.O.S. — CHAPTER #4

SHATTERING OLD SYSTEMS

Therefore, if anyone is in Christ, he is a new creation. The old has passed away; behold, the new has come. All this is from God, who through Christ reconciled us to himself And gave us the ministry of reconciliation;
— (2 Corinthians 5:17-18)

We've learned the benefits of de-cluttering our bed-rooms. Going hand-in-hand with this, we must learn to de-clutter our minds of lies. This means shattering your old systems of belief. Your old system of sexual intimacy is the way you've proceeded to achieve intimacy up to now. If you are sick of sex, then your old system is not working for you and must be shattered, struck down, and put away. After shattering the old, you must pick up the new.

Shattering your old systems will also require de-cluttering areas of your life that have run amuck. We must make our minds, attitudes, and schedules right.

De-cluttering your mind begins with a decision to not take the world's view of sexual intimacy. Go to your Heavenly Father and ask Him to take away this corrupted view. You are quickly changing how you think about sexual intimacy by asking for God's help. God shows us in scripture that David was a man after His heart (1 Samuel 13:14). In my opinion, David should be classified under "heathen." David did everything we deem wrong in the sight of God. But, when confronted with sin, David didn't try to explain why he did what he did; he went into immediate repentance and immediate obedience. Guess what? David's circumstances didn't change. The people in his life didn't change, but David was a new man. Repentance made him live with a new mind desiring to please God.

If you do not want to dwell on the sick of sex side of your relationship, you must be willing to immediately obey God and His Word. You must know that your old way of viewing sexual intimacy is incorrect and you must accept God's beautiful creation of sexual intimacy.

Remember being a little girl and your mother told you to do something? How many times did you not feel like doing it but yet you did? There are some things we do, everyday, that we just don't feel like doing. Yet we do them because they are either demanded of us to be done, or we must complete them out of necessity. You must choose to change your mind about sexual intimacy. It is a necessity.

Your husband may not change but if your mind has, he will look like a new man to you. Right now, God is asking you to renew your mind about intimacy. Your husband may not even be aware that this is an issue for you. But your renewing of your mind, changing the way you view intimacy will make intimacy reawaken for you. You will see intimacy and your husband differently. You may have been praying for your husband to change and for him to become a new man. If you renew your mind, he will look new to you, he will just have the same fingerprints.

To shatter old systems, choose to think about things the way God thinks about them. When you think about your husband, think about him the way God does. God cannot agree that your husband is a good-for-nothing-rascal that you would be better off without. He sees your husband in light of his relationship with Him. He is His son whom He loves.

God created the sexual relationship to be good. He wouldn't be able to think about sex between two married Christians, who desire to be obedient to Him and His Word, in a negative way. You have all the tools necessary (a personal relationship with Christ and a desire to obey Him and His Word) to have a "good" sex life. But you must be willing to shatter all of your old ways of thinking about sexual intimacy. The way to de-clutter your thinking is to renew your mind.

As a child in my family of origin, my parents had 4 daughters before me. My mom was very wise in getting us in the kitchen at a young age. She was known throughout Kansas City as a GREAT cook and was training us girls to follow suit. The only problem, being one of the younger kids, my opportunities to prepare a complete meal didn't come until I was out of the house. When I was home, I was given jobs like making the juice, putting the butter on the bread, setting the table, etc. I didn't have the chance to stuff the turkey or the pork chops, make meat loaf, cut up or fry the chicken. I was the side-dish queen.

As I grew, I did get more responsibility. I was given the task of making dressing one Sunday. Cooking like my mother (with no recipe) I added too much sage and my dressing was green. Even though it had good flavor, no one could get over the color and I was teased relentlessly. On another occasion, I was making a cake for dessert. Using real butter, I had no idea it needed to be softened to room temperature. I put the stick of butter into the mixer and it stuck between the blades. I used my finger to free the butter and my finger got stuck while the mixer was trying to mix. I let out a yell and my sister unplugged the mixer and saved my finger. (I added color and flavor to this cake with the blood that poured from my finger...I don't remember if we ate the cake). Everyone in the room laughed so hard, I began to believe cooking was just not my thing.

Living on my own years later, I begin to cook regularly, adding my own twists and spins to others recipes and making up some of my own. I would always have friends over who would compliment my cooking but they were starving singles, too, and I didn't believe them.

When I married Ray, he always complimented my cooking and compared mine to his mother's dishes. Ray helped me to believe I was a good cook. I renewed my mind with this correct information and not the unfortunate events of my past. With this renewed mind, eliminating the false information and replacing it with the truth, I have operated a catering business out of my home the last 20 years.

Even with this catering business and believing that I am a pretty good cook, I still must continually renew my mind and shatter the old system of thinking that cooking is not my thing. I have to run away from the voice that tells me my dishes are just mediocre.

The enemy of your martial intimacy will use this same type of low self-esteem with you. Maybe he has you feeling like you are not attractive to your husband, you are too heavy, you are too thin, you are too boisterous, quiet, long-legged, short-legged, too top heavy, bottom heavy, etc. But you must renew your mind with truth.

When Satan comes at us with the temptation to look at sex in any other light than what comes from God, the creator of sex, we must run with our minds and flee from the lies.

To flee the untruth, you must fill your mind with truth. If the enemy can get you to think negatively about sex with your husband and dwell there, his battle is won. We live where we dwell. Your dwelling place is your home. If you believe the lie that Satan has told you and have not replaced it with truth, you become an inhabitant of that lie. The lie becomes real to you and you begin to live like the lie is the truth.

If the enemy can get you to think negatively about sex with your husband and dwell there, his battle is won.

Philippians 4:4-9 says: "Finally, brothers, whatever is true, whatever is honorable, whatever is just, whatever is pure, whatever is lovely, whatever is commendable, if there is any excellence, if there is anything worthy of praise, think about these things. What you have learned and received and heard and seen in me-practice these things, and the God of peace will be with you."

It is so important that we begin to base our thoughts on the truth. God's Word is truth. Any thought that is contradictive to anything in the Word of God is false. A

70

lie. When Satan enters your mind with a lie regarding sex, you may even need to remind yourself of these truths:

> Satan: You know that your pitiful excuse of a husband is going to approach you tonight, just to meet HIS needs.

> You: *Whatever is true*. Is this a true statement? No. First of all, God doesn't see my husband as a pitiful excuse of a husband. God sees my husband as His perfect gift to me.

> Satan: Sex with him is only for his enjoyment. Truthfully, I don't believe he would know if you slipped out and had a woman off the street take your place.

> You: *Whatever is honorable*. Is this honorable? No. Secondly, this kind of thinking does not bring honor to God or to my marriage.

> Satan: I don't even know why you tolerate his advances. He is only wooing you to get what he wants.

> You: *Whatever is just, whatever is pure, whatever is lovely, whatever is commendable,*

if there be any excellence, if there is any thing worthy of praise, think about these things.

Satan: You know what I am saying is true.

You: No, this time I am going to believe God's Word. Paul said in Philippians 4:9, "What you have learned and received and heard and seen in me, practice these things, and the God of peace will be with you." I need some peace in my sexual relationship with my husband, so, *GET THEE BEHIND ME, SATAN!*

I hear ladies at conferences and churches say that Satan uses this same tactic over and over again. He has caused so much pain. How do we learn wisdom enough to not believe and obey Satan's voice?

Jesus, Himself, left us a clear illustration of what we must do when Satan comes at us with half-truths. First, we must know that Satan comes at us in areas that we are weak. Most of us have gotten the wrong information about sex, so he plays upon all that is wrong.

He tempted Jesus when He was weak. In Matthew 4, Jesus was led by the Spirit into the wilderness to be tempted by the Devil. After fasting for forty days and forty nights, He became hungry. The tempter came and said to Him, "If you are the Son of God, tell these stones to become loaves of bread." But he answered, "It is written, 'one must not live on bread alone, but on every word coming out of the mouth of God.'"

After this failed attempt, Satan tries to remind Jesus who He is and that He deserves more. He will do the same to you. He wants you to get into the selfish mode of thinking you are worthy of more and should demand more. Matthew 4:5-7 says, "Then the devil took him to the Holy City and had him stand on the highest point of the temple. He said to Jesus, "If you are the Son of God, throw yourself down. For it is written, "God will put his angels in charge of you,' and 'with their hands they will hold you up, so that you will never hit your foot against a rock.'" Jesus said to him, "'Again it is written, You shall not put the Lord your God to the test.'"

Satan also wants us to see all that we could have if obey him. He wants you to believe that things would be better if you "only trust him." But we must guard ourselves with the Word of God. You have to know and be willing to say to the enemy of your marital intimacy, "It is written, God's Word is a lamp unto my feet and a light unto my path." And frankly, "You shall not put me, a child of God, to the test!"

De-cluttering Your Attitude

De-cluttering your attitude is much harder than

de-cluttering your mind. It is easy to say you are going to change but doing it is more difficult. The only way to respond with the proper actions is to change your attitude. If you change the way you think about sexual intimacy, most times, that is only seen by you. But when you change your attitude about sex, it affects you and your husband. A right attitude about anything will produce right actions towards that very thing. Or, as portrayed in the movie *Facing the Giants*, "Your actions will always follow your beliefs."

In order to de-clutter our attitude, we must make a decision that may go against everything we feel to be true. The attitude that you have about sex wasn't just made in one day. It has taken years to establish this feeling. And you are probably comfortable with it. It feels safe and off limits. But, if you fully believed that, you probably wouldn't be reading this book.

I believe you are tired of feeling this way about sex because, for some reason, sex won't go away. Your husband continually wants sexual intimacy or you want sexual intimacy and your husband does not. So you are desperate to find a new way; a new attitude. Patti LaBelle said it best:

> "I'm feeling good from my head to my shoes. Know where I'm goin' and I know what to do. I've tidied up my point of view. I got a new attitude."

74

We need to tidy up our point of view. That begins with thinking about your husband and all that is right with him. Respond to your husband with that same attitude. This takes practice and obedience. If you practice doing that which is right, soon right becomes second nature to you. You end up doing "right" before you do wrong. And in order to focus on what is right; you must be willing to obey the Word of God immediately.

A right attitude about anything will produce right actions towards that very thing.

Too often our obedience to something takes us time to work it out, almost as if we need to contemplate whether or not we want to obey this time. Tidying up your point of view regarding sexual intimacy must mean thinking right about your husband—immediately. This is a major request because you probably have valid reasons for your hesitation.

But hesitation gives Satan the opportunity to give you another option and to consider another side. His other side is wrong. The only option to formulate a habit of thinking right about your husband and your intimacy is immediate obedience-thinking right (what is true) right away. Focus on the blessings that God has given you. Forget the things that are out of your control.

In Genesis 17:10; 15-17; 26-27, God made some promises to Abraham:

And God said to Abraham, "This is my covenant, which you shall keep, between me and you and your offspring after you: Every male among you shall be circumcised…" And God said to Abraham, "As for Sarai your wife, you shall not call her name Sarai, but Sarah shall be her name. I will bless her, and moreover, I will give you a son by her. That very day Abraham and his son Ishmael were circumcised. And all the men of his house, those born in the house and those bought with money from a foreigner, were circumcised with him.

God made a covenant with Abraham and told him to bear a sign of that covenant on himself and every male of his household. After God had finished talking with him, Abraham got up and took all who were in his household and immediately obeyed all that God told him to do. Abraham knew it would be painful for his entire household to obey God's command. But despite the pain, Abraham obeyed that very day.

You have made a covenant with God to love your husband, and you wear a sign of that covenant every day—your wedding ring, presented to you at the altar where the covenant was made. In order to become a woman who de-clutters her attitude, you must learn how to become an immediate obeyer. You have made a covenant with God and your husband. You have promised to love him until death do you part. Changing your attitude may cause you pain, but you must obey God. And the faster you obey, the easier it is to change your attitude.

An attitude is harder to change the longer you think about it. Thinking about it allows you a longer opportunity to change your actions, and it gives Satan more time to shoot his fiery arrows of lies at you.

When you choose to change your attitude about sex, the pain soon begins to fade away, and all that is left is the promise of the covenant. You will have less pain than if you chose not to obey. The pain that will result from disobedience is far greater and longer lasting than the pain of immediate obedience. If you immediately obey, you choose to do the right thing, and the right action takes place. Become an immediate obeyer and you change your attitude; thereby changing your mind about your entire intimate relationship with your husband.

There is another added bonus from obeying immediately. It is a new expression of joy. When you immediately obey, you understand that it is right before God, and you show joy. A Christian who knows they are doing the will of God, no matter how difficult, will display an underlying joy and peace.

If you keep succumbing to the wrong attitude, it eats at you, and you become a person no one wants to be around. A foul attitude in any area of your life will spill over to every other area sooner or later. Have you ever met a crabby old woman who complained about everything? It most likely began with one little negative attitude in her life that she didn't change.

Ray had a young cousin, Derek, who, at birth, was diagnosed with sickle cell anemia. Sickle cell is an inherited blood disorder characterized by hard and pointed red blood cells. The points of the cells result in painful episodes, infections, anemia; damage to body organs and early death. The sickle-shaped cells have a tendency to get stuck in blood vessels and block the flow of blood. This causes episodes of severe pain and damage to organs because of the lack of oxygen.

Derek had an extreme case of sick cell anemia and years of painful episodes. These episodes never gave him any warnings, and he lived day after day with pain.

We loved being around Derek and there was never any pity; Derek was always joyful. He was full of fun and always had a hilarious comment that made us all laugh. Even when his eyes were as yellow as daisies because of his Bilirubin levels, you could count on Derek to add laughter to your day.

I am certain that if Derek could have given the disease away, he would have. He knew that his life span was going to be shortened. He knew that he would not get to see his twelve-year-old daughter grow up, but Derek dwelt in joy because of his relationship with the Joy-Maker. Derek displayed joy until the day he died of sickle cell in the spring of 2007.

From the day he was born, Derek was given documentation and facts about the symptoms of what typical sickle cell disease looked like. He knew that his life would be a difficult one to live, but it was the life he was given. Derek determined to live with this illness, whether good or bad, and he determined it would not change his joy in life. He could have had a bad attitude (as some with chronic pain display) and we would all have understood. But he chose to take an attitude that allowed him to see life full of joy even though his circumstances said otherwise. He knew that he had no choice but to live with this ailment because God had chosen him to have it.

Marriage will occasionally be painful, but we can determine to live with joy until the end. We need to establish the truth of marriage in our hearts. Matthew 5:18, says, "But those things which proceed out of the mouth come forth from the heart; and they defile the man." Not only will the negative thoughts from your heart defile you as a woman but these thoughts will defile your marriage.

Genuine joy is not something that can be turned off or on. It is a state of being. To a person who owns true joy, even in the midst of pain or sorrow, there is hope on their lips and faces. People love to hang out with joyful people because they are real, and it offers hope for them.

To live with an attitude of hopelessness is to believe that your situation is beyond change. You can have peace in the midst of turmoil—just by changing your attitude. But your attitude change must have an anchor. The anchor of your attitude is Jesus.

Overcoming "Intimacy Indifference"

There is one very subtle illness that is killing many families in our society and it is called "Intimacy Indifference." It is an illness crippling our future generations, and we are allowing it to happen. Intimacy indifference is a threat to our legacies and it is fatal to our families if we do nothing about it. We need to get angry enough to put up our dukes and fight.

To accept intimacy indifference, you simply determine one day that this is as good as it gets and you begin believing that it is never going to get any better. You begin to live in that lie.

But you actually hold, in your hand, the key necessary to overcome the lie that is eating away at your family legacy: believing the Word of God.

One of the wisest verses is Proverbs 14:1: "The wise woman builds her house, but the foolish tears it down with her own hands." You must see your situation as despairing enough to realize that not changing it is tearing down your own house, brick by brick. It leaves you with no place to live, no roof to protect you, and rubble in your family core.

But an immediate attitude change affects the core of your family. It gives your family hope and new light. When your family has new light to shine on the right pathway, they reach their desired destination. So you must determine today, that you've had enough and want a new light shed on this situation of intimacy, a light of truth.

My dear friend, Candy called me one day and we began talking about this topic. Candy has been through many devastating things that have caused her much pain in her life. (You can find out about her story in her book, *Ransomed—A True Story of Freedom*.) Because of sexual abuse when she was a child, sexual intimacy was intimidating and unpleasant. She was actually afraid of it.

As Candy and I were talking, I began to share with her some of the information about de-cluttering your attitude. Candy listened with an occasional "hmm" like it was something she had never considered. She thanked me for sharing with her and went home only to call a few nights later ecstatic. She decided after twelve years of marriage, in order to de-clutter her attitude, she would buy her first negligee. In de-cluttering her attitude and purchasing a negligee, she made her actions obey her newfound attitude, and the result was a meaningful conversation about sex with her husband.

Sex is an uncomfortable subject for Candy and just a small change in her attitude allowed her conversation to be different than ever before. I am sure this is and will be the first of many conversations for Candy and her husband.

The enemy will try to prevent these conversations from happening because he knows that intimate conversation will produce intimacy. When you de-clutter your attitude, you must de-clutter it daily until the attitude that you used to have is a distant memory.

What's Next? De-cluttering Our Schedules

The final thing that has to change is your priorities. In order to develop a sexually fulfilling relationship, you must get to the place where sex is a priority. Sex cannot be prioritized unless you have invested time in intimacy with your husband. To not invest in conversation, fun, and life with your husband would be as if you are having sex with a stranger at night.

Remember when you met your best girlfriend? You liked her and wanted to get to know her better. You made time to spend with her. It was not a time you dreaded; it was very pleasant.

The same has to be done with your husband. You need to prioritize your schedule to spend enjoyable time with your husband. You know you are too busy when you dread going on a date with him because you are too tired or think he is not pleasant company.

When is the last time you asked your husband an arbitrary question and really wanted to hear his response? Recently I asked Ray if someone gave us a million dollars, how he would spend it. He spouted off a couple of ideas and then went on to something else. About three days later, he came back and said, "I changed my mind about the million dollars." Then he listed off more things he would do with the money. We had fun laughing and dreaming like the one million bucks was in our bank account.

When Ray and I were first married, we loved to talk to each other. Ray would follow me around and talk to me while I cleaned the kitchen. Occasionally, I would stop what I was doing and look at him, but I usually just kept cleaning. (There was never a spot of spaghetti sauce left under the knobs on my stove.) One day I noticed that I was the only one in the kitchen. I had chosen a clean kitchen over conversation with my husband. It didn't take me long to realize that the kitchen could wait, but conversation may not.

Busyness keeps us from looking at our husband and allowing him to talk to us undistracted. Some of us will have to draw our husbands out of their quiet places (work, TV, spending time online). They need to know that they are safe talking about their thoughts, feelings, and fears with us. You need to know his heart, and you desperately need him to know yours.

Remember your dating days? Sitting beside your boyfriend and holding his hand was what you lived for. Well, this boyfriend is now your husband and he still needs those couch cuddles. You need to slow down enough to sit by him and drink in his smell, hold his hand, and talk. It has become so easy for us to get comfortable with our husbands that we have forgotten to continue to invest in our relationship. To shatter old systems, the continual investment must last a lifetime. Otherwise Satan will make sure to allow your old way of doing marriage and intimacy to creep back into the forefront of your relationship. We must prioritize de-cluttering those things in our lives that are not true. We must not allow our schedules to run us. We must make sure that God's Word is what we use as the standard. It will always bring us to a safe, truth-abiding place.

> *We were buried therefore with him by baptism into death, In order that, just as Christ was raised from the dead by the glory of the*

Father, We too might walk in newness of life.
— (Romans 6:4)

JOURVOTIONAL

Shattering Old Systems

1. Name some things you have heard or seen regarding sexual intimacy that you know are lies (from T.V., relationships you have observed, conversations you have been a part of, etc.)

_____

_____

_____

2. What are some old systems of belief that you perceived to be true that you know need to be shattered?

_____

_____

_____

3. List some of the things in your mind that you have taken on from the world's view of intimacy. Then spend time in prayer, right now, to ask God to take away these incorrect views.

4. Just as David had to repent of his sin in order live forgiven, you, too, must have a time of repentance of the areas you need to change. Write down these areas and spend time in prayer with your Heavenly Father, taking each of these things to Him. He is the only one who can change or initiate transformation.

_____

_____

_____

5. What are some of the things you remember your parents telling you to do that you didn't want to do, but now as an adult you know they are necessities? (ex. taking out the trash)

_____

_____

_____

_____

6. What are some areas or thoughts about intimacy that you know you need to change?

_____

_____

_____

_____

7. How do you think God sees these areas or thoughts?

_____

_____

_____

8. In order to de-clutter your mind, there are some areas, thoughts, or duties you must run from immediately when they arise. What are these areas, thoughts, or duties?

_____

_____

_____

9. Read Philippians 4:4-9 in this chapter again and answer these questions regarding your intimacy with your husband:

· What is true about your marriage?

_____

_____

_____

· What is honorable about your marriage?

_____

_____

_____

· What is just (right) about your marriage?

_____

_____

_____

_____

· What is pure about your marriage?

_____

_____

_____

_____

· How often are you focusing on the things you have just written?

_____

_____

10. When you think about your attitude regarding sexual intimacy, what are the issues in your attitude that need to be tidied up?

_____

_____

_____

_____

11. Can you think of a person in your life who has unpleasant circumstances, yet they exude joy? If so, write a little about what you have observed.

_____

_____

_____

_____

_____

12. Read 1 Corinthians 10:13 again and soak in the middle of that verse: "God is faithful, and he will not let you be tempted beyond your ability." Our temptation would be to allow our intimacy to remain mundane and slip into mediocrity. What are some things you can do now to change your view of sex?

_____

_____

_____

_____

_____

_____

_____

_____

_____

13. What are some things you can eliminate now in your schedule so you can refocus your time, attention, and energy to your marriage and intimacy with your husband?

_____

_____

_____

Ways to Begin to Shatter Old Systems

1. Write truth cards and carry them with you. (Write the lie on one side of an index card and the truth on the other. Use God's word to find truth)

2. Write five truth-filled statements and meditate on them.

3. Make a schedule eliminator list and tape it to your bathroom mirror. Remind yourself every morning that your intimacy is more important than your schedule.

4. Memorize Jeremiah 32:17 and Jeremiah 32:27.

S.O.S. — CHAPTER #5

SHAMED OF SHAPE

Even every one that is called by my name:
For I have created him for my glory, I have
formed him; yea, I have made him.
— (Isaiah 43:7)

91

As a speaker at the FamilyLife "Weekend to Remember" conferences, there have been only three occasions in fifteen years where I was not the only female speaker. On one such event, Luci Stanley was asked to give the "wife" session, and I was elected to do the "mom" session. (I wonder why?)

As I sat in on Luci's session, she said something that really hit home. "Too many of us are ashamed of our shapes. We tell our husbands, "I hate this, but you love it." I am sure many of us walk around thinking that very thing. We might not say those words out loud, but we say them every time we see ourselves, unclothed, in a full-length mirror.

I remember being around eleven or twelve years old and needing a beginner's bra. My older sister needed one also. My mom bought us both size 30A. I will never forget that day because I was so proud to own my first bra. After all, at the ripe age of twelve, I was a maturing woman.

And mature I did. A year later, my younger sister and I took school pictures together. I wore a white turtleneck with a bluish-green scarf tied around my neck, and I brought out one of my trusty 30A bras to wear. Unfortunately for me, I had gone from a 30A to a 32DD in one year. My mom was very busy with ten children and the extra responsibilities of being a pastor's wife. I didn't realize that the bra was that small and no one noticed my rather rapid growth spurt until I got the school pictures back. No one who looked at those pictures ever noticed our faces—only the rest of my breasts hanging out of the sides of that little 30A bra. I was so ashamed.

Needless to say, my mother told me I was built like "those Campbells" on my father's side. She then introduced me to full-figured bras.

Three immediate downers for a thirteen year old:

> 1. I was bigger in one place than my sister almost two years my senior.
>
> 2. My mom said I was "full-figured." What did that mean to me? Fat!
>
> 3. I was "built like the Campbells." No girl wants her breasts compared to her father's family.

That started the downfall of my self-esteem and of hating a part of me that I, at that point, could not change. As a cheerleader in junior high and high school, after every jump, I felt like I had to wait on the ripple effect of those big breasts to stop jumping after I hit the floor. By the time I graduated from high school, those 32DDs had grown to whopping 34DDDs. And for a 122-pound, 5'4" inch girl...something was way out of proportion.

Those became my "hide the breasts" days—big sweatshirts and nothing clingy or tight. No fitted t-shirts in public. Never accentuate what you hate about yourself, right?

Now advance fourteen years and I am twenty-six years old getting ready to marry my best friend. Ray likes, no, *loves*, the way God has blessed me in that certain area. So here is this man who has obeyed the Lord and kept himself pure for marriage, thinking, "Thank you, Lord, for blessing me with a *blessed* wife." And I am thinking, "Do wedding dresses and negligees come in sweatshirt fabric?"

Thus began the beginning of my diving lessons. No, not into a swimming pool. Diving into bed before my husband comes into the bedroom. Pulling the covers up over my neck so he can't see me in the light. I was an expert diver. I even waited until the lights were out to go use the restroom.

Freedom Comes

A couple of years ago, I was home watching the *Discovery Channel* and saw several ladies going through breast augmentation surgery. One lady was ashamed of the size of her breasts and hid them in big sweatshirts and wore nothing tight. It was much the same scenario, but she was a size 30A. What? All those years I had been hiding something God had naturally given to me. Millions of ladies are paying *thousands* of dollars to get what was given to me in just one year's growth, and I hated them!

Well, who was duped all those years? Remember when Ray thanked God on his wedding day for his blessed wife? I am no longer a diver but a skinny dipper. I wait around painting my toenails until Ray comes in the room. Then I publicly (in the privacy of my bedroom, of course) take off my shirt and bra…then look for a night gown. Oh, and on occasion, I prance myself into the bathroom and back to the closet like I have forgotten something. He loves this show, and it is for his eyes only!

A lot of women are spending a fortune changing something about their bodies, so they will look better and feel better (or at least, they *think*). We absolutely must get to a point where we appreciate the unique bodies God has given to us! (And unique they are…no two are alike.)

Contentment Is Freedom

Find yourself content with your lot and you will experience true freedom. You must first know that in order to become content, you must be thankful. Remember at twelve when I was so happy to be a maturing woman? That was before the stigma of being "full-figured" set in.

When we are referred to as a "mature Christian," we appreciate the observation. We love it when people come to us to get mature advice. But, how many of us would go to the market and pick out immature fruit? I don't know about you, but I look for the biggest watermelon in the bin when I'm shopping. I feel that I am a frugal shopper if I can get the bigger one for the same price as the smaller one. Not one of us would pick small, immature fruit. We would rather pass up fruit than select under ripe ones.

I believe we have been consumed with staying in shape and thinking that staying in shape means being the shape we were when we were young and fit. We do need to be fit but we need to view our bodies as mature. We need to stop spending so much time trying to regain that immature girlish figure and become content with our mature figures. I am not saying that we should not exercise. Exercising does more for the parts of your body that you cannot see than the parts you can. Ever wonder why that man you always see at the fitness center pumping tons of iron still has love handles? It's not all about the love handles, it's about his heart.

We must not only accept and be content with the body God has given us, but the shape that he has uniquely given to us. Some of our husbands have landed the more mature piece of fruit in the bin, and we are saying to him, "Throw me back." No, he along with the guidance of God has handpicked you and both are very content with His selection.

By not accepting our shapes it causes us to have negative feeling about our bodies. We do whatever it takes to bring as little attention to ourselves as possible. Even in the privacy of our bedroom with our husbands, we don't want much attention. Negative feelings about our bodies cause us to view intimacy negatively.

After moving to Tennessee, the pastor of our new church was doing a series on the Book of Hebrews. His title was *Grow up! It's all about JESUS!* He told us that the Hebrews were discontent and were ready to give up on their faith in God. The writer of the book was telling them to grow up. It is not about you anyways; it is all about Jesus.

Have you noticed how one thing that you deem a problem in your life can affect your whole perspective? If you are not content with your shape, it will affect another part of your life. You cannot leave your shape behind. Even if you add more clothing to cover it up, you will still experience discontentment. You will begin to view your life based on how you feel about yourself.

Ever had an issue with someone in your church? The more this issue stays unresolved, the more everything about the church will seem bad. Some of us will think we need to find a new church; others of us will avoid contact with this person. If this person enters a room, we all of the sudden have to go to the restroom, whether we need to go or not.

When someone on the job constantly gets under our skin, many times this can cause us to have a problem with the job itself and makes us consider finding a new job. We even eat lunch at our desks instead of going to the lunchroom if it means we have to come in contact with the particular person who has offended us.

What we are doing is something my mom called "cutting off our noses to spite our face" or "throwing the baby out with bath water." Our discontentment causes us to see only the negative. Our responses are made out of the "bad" view. If we are discontent with our bodies, we cast a negative view on anything that has to do with our appearance. We hate picking out clothes; we hate eating in front of people; and we are always thinking about how this or that is going to contribute to the shape of our bodies. We become consumed with the very thing we hate. We don't even like others to touch these bodies that we hate.

Our husbands are in a predicament. They come to give us a hug, and we think, "I hope he doesn't notice all the squishy cellulite." Your husband can sense that hesitation, and after time, hugs are no more. He feels like he is the reason you are so distant in your embrace. This discontentment of our bodies causes us to spend more time concerned about ourselves, and we don't even realize that we are becoming totally self-focused. Sexual freedom comes by being other-focused. It is not about you; it's about pleasing Jesus. And by pleasing Jesus and becoming other-focused, your husband is well-pleased.

A marriage that brings glory to God pleases Him. By focusing on pleasing your husband—not by resignation—you glorify God.

We need to be thankful to God for two working legs and forget about the spider veins. Thank Him for a stomach that can digest good food with no tubes inserted. Thank Him for the added bonus of that extra, middle roll.

Be thankful for a husband who is interested in being with you in a sexual way. This man desires to be with you intimately. Get over your shape and desire to be with him because life is too short to spend so much time focusing on what affects you and not striving to make the most of your relationship.

Sexual freedom comes by being other-focused.

In Song of Solomon, we read about a love affair between Solomon and his Shulamite wife. They carefully take the time to tell each other how much they love one another and all they love about each other. Every time I read this passage, I think that his woman must have been some foxy lady. The way her husband describes her, she must have been something to look at—a babe. I found myself wondering if she had an issue with any parts of her body. Listen to the way Solomon describes her belly: "your stomach is like a pile of wheat surrounded with lilies."

Solomon compares every part of her body to what it reminds him of most. "Your breasts are like two fawns, twins of the gazelle that graze among the lilies" (Song of

Solomon 4:5). His wife probably thought negatively about her "big belly" until Solomon said it was fenced about with lilies. She was like a Hawaiian woman with a lilied lei placed around her belly, and to Solomon, it was beautiful.

Now think about how this impacted this wife's image of herself. I can hear her now, "I might have a pile of wheat for my belly, but you, my man Solomon, can climb on for a hayride. Giddy-Up!"

God is creative in everything He creates. Everything has variety; everything has a different shape, color, and purpose. We look at our bodies and think they have to be like the woman next to us, or like models in a magazine. But we do not have the same body type. Some of the models don't even have that body type! (Photoshop has given them a simulated body and we think it is real.) God never intended two of His creations to be identical in any way, shape, or form. (Even my identical twin brothers are not exactly the same.)

In order to change the way you look at your body, you must quit looking at it and comparing it to others. Be thankful to God for giving your unique body to you. Once again, thankfulness is the doorway to contentment. Open that door and find freedom in intimacy.

God has formed our bodies and shapes. He created us and his work is wonderful. Psalm 139:13-15 says, "For you created my inmost being; you knit me together in my mother's womb. I praise you because I am fearfully and wonderfully made; your works are wonderful, I know that full well. My frame was not hidden from you when I was made in the secret place. When I was woven together in the depths of the earth, your eyes saw my unformed body. All the days ordained for me were written in your book before one of them came to be."

We must get to the place where we see our bodies as created by God. We have to see God's creativity and love as He made us. He wanted us to be unique. There is contentment in knowing this truth. God formed us and created us and His works are wonderful. When God completed creation on the sixth day, He announced that it was good, and He rested from His work. God sees His creation as good.

If we cannot enjoy a good, intimate relationship with our husbands because we are ashamed of our shape, we must focus on the Creator and Sustainer of our lives. God said all that He created was good. You are taking the focus off God when you focus on your shape, your lack or excess of parts, or if you focus on the image of others around you.

The enemy wants us to take the focus off God and place it on ourselves. Anytime you remove your focus from God in any area, the enemy uses the new focal point to remove your godly testimony. Satan takes the focus off God and purposes for us to become self-focused and motivated by what is important to us. Anything that is motivated by us is not bringing glory to God and, thereby, is not being used for its intended purposes.

Every time we come to God, He sees His child, created in His image. He isn't even affected by all that we see. When we look in a mirror, we see all our flaws. We often

When He looks at us, He sees all that is beautiful about us, and all that He created. We are accepted with complete approval.

turn away so that we don't have to look at ourselves. We have been tricked into thinking that all God sees are our flaws when we approach Him. But when He looks at us, He sees all that is beautiful about us, and all that He created. We are accepted with complete approval.

Because of our rejection of our bodies, we approach our husbands with a rejected view of ourselves. We place this rejection on him and in some ways, we even see him rejecting us. But God has a way of allowing your husband to see your body with no flaws. Or maybe the flaws are way less important to him. When we learn to live in the light of God's approval of us, we will begin to experience a new level of intimacy with our husbands.

Not every husband has the ability to accept and see us the way God does. Becoming more confident in who you are in Christ will allow your husband room to become more like Christ. As your husband grows, he will begin viewing you as Christ views you. He will become more concerned about your spiritual growth than the growth of any part of your body.

When you are viewed as Christ sees you, you are not worried about too many things. You understand grace and mercy because it has been granted to you. You will respond differently around a person who sees you like Christ does. That person is concerned about your relationship with the Lord more than anything else. That person (your spouse) will become the one person with whom you will be completely free, with no holding back. He grants you freedom by total acceptance.

Being totally accepted brings contentment. The benefit of being content, sexually, will change you from being Shamed of Shape to being Stupendously, Outrageously Sexy.

Your husband better watch out because it ain't Santa Claus coming to town; it's a whole new, free you!

JOURVOTIONAL

Shamed of Shape

1. What area of your body or body part would you change if you were given a magic potion? And why?

_____

_____

_____

_____

_____

2. What are some of the ways you try to hide or draw less attention to a body part or your entire body?

_____

_____

_____

_____

3. When you look around at the creativity of our Heavenly Father, list all the ways you see this body part you listed in #1 created on others around you.

_____

_____

_____

_____

_____

4. Looking at how creative God is, can you accept your body or body part as an object of His wonderful creativity? What would accepting this view do to your attitude?

_____

_____

_____

5. Do you feel like you spend too much time focusing on the things of importance that affect your life and not on the things of God? If so, list some of those things.

_____

_____

_____

6. Spend a minute or two in prayer thanking God for His creativity and for this body or body part that you may want to reject.

7. Read Isaiah 43:7. Why did God create you?

_____

_____

_____

_____

_____

Remember, when you understand the purpose for your creation, the details aren't quite as important. God has formed you and yes, has made you.

S.O.S. — CHAPTER #6

SHARE OUR STORIES: DORCAS

"We should not be ashamed to talk about what God wasn't ashamed to create."
— Howard Hendricks

Growing up, my family was very close. It was overall a good family consisting of my mother, step-father (who I called dad), and 6 siblings. My father died in a car accident before I was 2, but my step-father loved me as his own.

We had a wonderful home life; mom stayed at home and took care of us. My siblings and I were involved in church. My mother and dad did not go, early on, but we would walk with Aunt Beatrice and when Aunt Beatrice walked in front of the house, we'd better be ready.

I learned many scriptures at church and at the age of nine, I understood that I was a sinner and needed a Savior. I knew, even at that age, I was born to be a missionary and share the good news of Jesus.

On the night of my baptism, my mother surrendered her life to Christ and a week later my dad accepted Christ. Our household drastically changed. My parents begin living a passionate life for the Lord.

I hung out with my older sisters quite often. I remember their conversations about boys and even saw one of them let a boy touch her breasts. It made me so uncomfortable but I never talked about it.

In our home, sex was never mentioned. Growing up in the '60s, free sex was the message outside of our home. The message inside was "better not go out there and get pregnant." But there was no discussion. When I was a little older, my mother came to me and said, "if you need birth control pills, tell me." Without discussion or conversation, I was left to form my own opinion and the message I formulated was "it must be okay to have sex, just don't get pregnant."

I distinctly remember being so confused with the message that was before me sexually. I knew my mother had 3 babies before she was married (she had been involved with a married man). One of my sisters had gotten pregnant, and over the years there were many "good" girls in church I watched become pregnant. Confusing messages were all around me. At church, the Bible teaching was "do not fornicate" but every message around me was saying the exact opposite.

My dad said two things about sex that I will always remember, "A man will spill his seed anywhere" and "A Christian man will always walk away." I hid these two things in my heart.

At sixteen, I had a boyfriend. He was four years older than I was. Dad didn't think it was okay for me to see him but he nor mom ever said I couldn't so I did. One day, I approached my mom as she sat at the dining room table, "I think I need to go to the doctor," I said to her. "I think I'm ready to go." We both understood and she took me soon thereafter.

There was no conversation on the way there, no conversation as we set in the exam room, no conversation on the way back home. I am sure my mother sat beside me in turmoil as she didn't know what to say or how to express what she may have wanted to say.

Shortly thereafter, I had my first sexual experience with my boyfriend. It was so unpleasant. I remember feeling nothing but shame and pain. I felt as if I couldn't tell anyone. So, I just didn't see him anymore.

I became a very promiscuous teen and each time I had sex, I thought, "What's so good about this thing? I don't want to be here. There is nothing good about this!" I remember always feeling dirty afterwards and never wanting any light in the room. I didn't want them to see me.

I liked each guy until sex…then, I didn't like them or see them anymore. But when I met Charles, it was different. I remember the very first time I saw him. He was driving his white Eldorado with the striking red interior. We danced all night. He was easy to talk to and so handsome. I lived in Ohio at the time, but would come to Indianapolis every weekend to be with him.

One night when we were dancing, one of his friends came up to him and whispered, "Someone said your old lady is outside." I overheard the conversation. When I asked him if he was married, he said, "no." He later told me that he lived with this lady but they were going to break up.

My relationship with him grew and soon we were sexually involved. It was different than ever before. I liked it. I loved this man and that had to be the missing ingredient.

I began spending time with his family and his sister was the one who broke the news to me. "Charles is married! Did he tell you he was married?" But by this point, I was so in love, I kept seeing him. I was breaking my own conviction never to date a married man. So, I moved to Indianapolis and believed all his lies.

I stayed with Charles for three years and had a child. It was during the pregnancy that I realized he was not just coming and going home to his wife and children. He had another girlfriend on the side. I felt so betrayed. That left me alone and a single mother. But God who promised never to leave me or forsake me allowed these circumstances in my life to open my heart back to Him.

After having my baby, I went home to my mom and dad to stay for the 6 weeks following delivery. I so desired to rekindle my relationship with God and home was just the place to do so.

At my parent's home, I rededicated my life to Christ and desired to walk with the Lord. I met a Christian man in the church we were attending. He wanted to be sexually involved but I didn't want to. Then one day after relenting and having sex with him, I broke off the relationship because he was hindering my relationship with the Lord. But, I was pregnant again.

At this point in my life, I realized God was a God of redemption. I was in a church where the Word of God was not being taught. There was no accountability to the Word and I knew as long as I remained there, I would continue to compromise sexually.

God's Word became breath to me and my favorite scripture was "trust in the Lord with all your heart, and do not lean on your own understanding. In all your ways acknowledge him, and he will make straight your paths. Be not wise in your own eyes; fear the Lord, and turn away from evil. It will be healing to your flesh and refreshment to your bones" (Proverbs 3:3-8).

I knew that because of the choices I had made, I had stolen something from my children that could never be replaced. They were growing up without their fathers. I also knew that God would never forsake me, but there are consequences to sin that must be played out.

I immediately placed myself under the protection of my dad. Even being a grown woman with two small daughters and not living in my father's home, I began looking to my dad for direction. This meant a new church home, new accountability, a new lifestyle, and a new life. For the first time in my life, I was in the Word on a daily basis and teaching my children the Bible at home.

After some time, I began to desire a husband and I shared this with my dad. I told him, "Dad, there's nobody out there." And my dad said, "What about David?" I laughed.

David was a divorced dad at our church. He was not my type at all. Yes, he was tall and that was a plus but he was so quiet, very laid back, and had no aspirations for corporate America, whatsoever. I was very much into climbing the corporate ladder. David was going to Bible College and didn't seem to care how he dressed.

Forming a new singles ministry at our church, the pastor selected both David and I to be a part of the leadership committee. David was perfect for this leadership team because this church believed no divorce, no remarriage, no exceptions. He would be aiding to form a ministry in this new church that he would always be a part of.

Being a single mom on the team, most leadership meetings were held at my home where I could put my girls to bed. The team was put into pairs to pray about the direction of the ministry and David and I were paired into a team. He began staying around and soon a great friendship developed as we both were becoming more drawn to one another.

David wouldn't kiss me or put his arms around me. This was the most different relationship I had ever had. There were never any sexual overtones or advances. There were occasions were David would leave quickly at odd times and I soon knew he had the same commitment of celibacy that I now had. There was one occasion where I remembered clearly what my dad had said to me early on, "A Christian man will always walk away," and I knew for the first time I was in the presence of a Christian man who desired to please the Lord more than his own sexual desires.

After seeing each other almost one year, David and I knew something must change. He asked my dad if he could marry me and we have been happily married for 20 years.

***

Dorcas knew not only that David was trustworthy (he had only shown trust by not ever approaching her sexually prior to marriage) but God was trustworthy. David and Dorcas have walked hand in hand with God, every day, since the wedding.

The enemy still tries to flood her with doubt, fear, and mistrust. Dorcas told me there are times when she struggles with intimacy with David. She combats feeling dirty, dealing with thoughts from before marriage, and flashbacks of things that have happened. These attacks by Satan cause her to battle often with trust. Dorcas fights these battles by knowing, "When I am willing to please my Lord, then I am willing to please my husband."

She is a living witness of a transformed life. Not only from the woman she was prior to marriage, but she is experiencing freedom in marriage.

The enemy of marriage has attacked everyone who is married. He will use all the things that have plagued you and your husband prior to marriage to get you to respond to marriage and intimacy negatively. But Dorcas is one witness, daily choosing to wave the victory flag that comes from a surrendered life to Christ.

JOURVOTIONAL

Share Our Stories: Dorcas

1. Our first view of intimacy is formulated in our homes of origin. Where did your parents get their view of intimacy?

_____

_____

_____

_____

2. If your parents are Christians, do you know their stories of their salvation experience? Briefly write them down.

_____

_____

_____

_____

_____

_____

_____

3. If you had siblings, how did they portray intimacy with their boyfriends in front of you and others? (If no siblings, answer this regarding your closest friend).

_____

_____

_____

4. In your home growing up, was sex openly talked about, embarrassed conversation, or no news is good news?

_____

_____

5. How was your opinion formed about sexual intimacy while growing up?

_____

_____

_____

6. Dorcus did not want to be involved with a married man because she had witnessed the affects of it in her mom's life. What are some things that have affected you because of your parent's sexual history or their choices prior to marriage?

_____

_____

_____

_____

7. What are some of your own personal choices, prior to marriage, that you would change if you knew then what you know now?

_____

_____

_____

_____

8. Read Proverbs 3:3-8. Write out some ways that you may not have trusted in the Lord and have leaned on your own understanding in your own sexual history.

_____

_____

_____

9. Our Father is a Healer. He heals our wounds and straightens our mistakes. Write out your prayer to Him.

_____

_____

_____

_____

S.O.S. — CHAPTER #7

SAVE OUR SENSUALITY

His arms are rods of gold, set with jewels. His body is polished ivory, bedecked with sapphires. He legs are alabaster columns, set on bases of gold. — (Song of Solomon 5:14-15)

We must understand our need to be desired, for every one of us has a similar desire. We want to belong. We want an association with others.

As infants, we call it mimicking.
As teenagers, we call it being in the in crowd.
As adults, we call it connecting.

We want to have associations with others that make us feel accepted. It is an innate desire that even showed Adam that the animals just were not enough. Adam gave names to all the cattle and to the fowl of the air, and to

117

every beast of the field, but Adam did not find a helpmate among them (Genesis 2:20). The ole pooch just wasn't enough.

We long to be able to bear our souls to the person who knows us as well as, or even better than, we know ourselves. We want to share the stuff that happens to us with a person we can see and touch. We desire association, connectivity, and someone who loves us.

Anyone who does not desire this is called a hermit—a social recluse—and no one wants to be around them. The hermit is thankful, because he has no desire for socialization. But God created this inherent need in us to want intimacy. Just think if everyone were a hermit, humanity would no longer exist.

When I was in high school, most of my friends had boyfriends. I desired one too and my friends kept assuring me "your day will come." I've had friends who would cry themselves to sleep wondering why no one was interested in them. You have probably had similar experiences yourself or with your friends.

Now you are married to a man who desires to be with you every day for the rest of your life. He has made a vow before God and all his family. You made the same vow. Now you have this unique special relationship between you two, and you long to be desired by him. What? Yes, you long to be desired by him, not just physically, but for him to really know you.

SAVE OUR SENSUALITY

It's called lust if you only care to be desired physically. But both of you desire a relationship. You and he desire to know each other better than anyone else in the world.

Sensuality Is a Divine Right with Our Husbands

My mom told me all the things "fast girls" would do because she wanted me to avoid sexual involvement until marriage. Unfortunately, these ideas put in our heads by our parents of things we should not do make us think certain things are flat out wrong, even in marriage. We have become prudes, even in our own marriage beds.

We were told that sensuality, prior to marriage, is wrong, but do you know you have the right to be sensual with your husband? God gives you permission to grant your own husband sexual pleasure. In becoming a sensual woman with your husband, you and your husband become satisfied sexually. In Song of Solomon 2:7, 3:5, and 8:4, it warns us not to awaken love before its time. But when it is time, this entire book of the Bible allows us to see that nothing sensual about the body is off limits. You can stir up love, heat it, bake it, and eat it. Love, in marriage, is right and should be stirred up, often.

According to Webster's dictionary, sensual means relating to or consisting in gratification of the senses or the indulgence of appetite. To be sensual with your

119

husband is to give him an appetite for sexual intimacy. Generally, a man's appetite for sex doesn't take much preparation. He is ready for dessert when you have only shown him the appetizer! But by taking the time to indulge his senses, you are preparing him to have an appetite for intimacy. You prepare your own appetite for it, as well. After all, preparation for sexual intimacy is mostly for you.

When you have purposed to feel sensual and sexy, it prepares you for intimacy, and you desire to physically be with your husband.

For most women, it takes time for us to be prepared for the sex act. We need foreplay. We need the time to unwind, let go of all the things we have on our minds and get in the mood. Sensuality or being sensual is getting us in the mood. Sensuality will look different to each of us but we know what our triggers are to prepare us for intimacy that is pleasing to both us and our husbands.

Have you ever been at an event where a sexy woman enters the room? You can tell by the way she walks that she is aware of her beauty and charm. Every man (and woman) in the room is aware of her style. In the same way, as you enter your bedroom, your sensuality (your style, beauty, charm) should draw your husband's attention completely to you. When you *have purposed* to feel sensual and sexy, it prepares you for intimacy, and you desire to physically be with your husband. Your husband desires and deserves a wife who is sensual in the privacy of your bedroom. Sexual pleasure is a divine right for us and our husbands, and we have the right to be givers and partakers of this pleasure.

Sensuality Is a Step Toward Freedom

There is such freedom in being sexually unhindered with your husband. You have nothing to hide or be ashamed of. This is the point where you must realize that momma was trying to protect your innocence prior to marriage but it is okay for you to enjoy the pleasures of sexual intimacy with your husband. You understand what it means to be "naked and unashamed" (Genesis 2:25). Sensuality is freedom.

If you allow yourself to grant sexual pleasure to your husband, you give yourself permission to be sexually gratified. Sensuality takes all the agendas and selfishness out of sex and allows you to grant your husband a pleasurable gift.

When you give a gift (and you are giving this gift from the heart), you have no expectations of the receiver. When that gift is genuine, it is given from a pure heart, and you give it because you wanted to offer it. We need to purpose in our hearts to give our husbands the gift of sexual pleasure. We need to give this gift with no expectations to us. It must be given from a heart of gratitude for the gift of intimacy.

A lot of women desire to offer unhindered, sexual pleasure to their husbands but feel their gift is already rejected prior to giving it. When we get to the place where we not only are free to be sensual but can offer our bodies intimately to our husbands, then we are at the place where God is being glorified in our sexual intimacy. That must be our ultimate goal.

Sexual intimacy before marriage is sin. It defrauds those who are participants in the act because it doesn't honor God, the Creator of the act. If you are one of the many women who have participated in pre-marital sex, you have been defrauded by the enemy and you must make a commitment to never to fall for sexual fraud again. Our Heavenly Father is a God of restoration and hope. One of my friends was actively involved in pre-marital sex and made a commitment to not have sex until she was married. After marrying and returning from her honeymoon, she told me, "It was like I had never had sex before!" That is what God does. He restores your purity so you view sex in a different light. Sexual sensuality can be restored in marriage and is a gift you give. It is a launching pad for a satisfying sexual relationship.

Sexual sensuality in marriage is where both husband and wife have an appetite for the act of sexual intimacy and desire to please each other. To be sensual in your bedroom will make you feel sexy and whets your appetite for sex. In finding sensuality and creating an appetite for sexual intimacy, you find your soul mate. You find your connection and where you belong.

> *Let him kiss me with the kisses of his mouth!*
> *For your love is better than wine;* — (Song
> of Solomon 1:2)

JOURVOTIONAL

Save Our Sensuality

1. What are some of the groups, churches, organization, clubs, or sororities that you belonged to at one time or another?

_____

_____

_____

_____

2. What were some of your reasons for joining these groups?

_____

_____

_____

3. Make of list of the "wisdom" and advice you were given by your mother, father, or older women to try to keep you from becoming involved sexually prior to marriage.

_____

_____

_____

_____

_____

_____

_____

4. In Genesis 2:25, what do you think being "naked and unashamed" means?

_____

_____

_____

5. In this chapter, it states that sensuality takes the selfishness out of sex. Why is sensuality necessary in sexual intimacy?

_____

_____

_____

_____

6. What one thing in life brings you the most pleasure?

_____

_____

_____

7. Is intimacy with your husband more pleasurable than this thing? _____

8. Read Song of Solomon 1:2 and add your pleasurable thing in the blank. Let him kiss me with the kisses of his mouth! For your love is better than _____.

Ways to Begin Restoration of Your Sensuality

1. Simple love notes sent anonymously to your husband (you may choose to drench it in perfume).

2. Fun, romantic cards left for him to find - no special occasion necessary.

3. Spend time praying that God will begin to set you free to be sensual and give you creative ideas that you can begin to do. When God gives you an idea—DO IT!

4. Simply Romantic Nights, FamilyLifeResource Kit.

S.O.S. — CHAPTER #8

SANCTIFICATION OR SIN?

...for thou hast created all things, and for thy pleasure they are and were created.
— (Revelation 4:11)

Can you remember the very first time you heard or understood the word sex? Did you want to hide, blush, or did you desire it in the future for yourself? Most of us wake up one day and find that we have been stained with a wrong introduction to sexual intimacy.

I abhor oatmeal. When I was a little girl, my mother would make me eat oatmeal because it was good for me. Every time, I would puke it up and it would spoil oatmeal for my brothers and sisters.

Ray loves oatmeal. He takes his time adding the right about of butter and sugar until it is perfect. Then he sits down to dive into it like it is his requested last meal.

Because of my first introductions to oatmeal, I doubt it will ever appeal to me. The only way oatmeal will appeal to me is that I change the way I think about oatmeal. I now have to look at oatmeal for all the benefits it gives me. I must think about the benefits of it being a valuable fiber for me. The fiber in oatmeal is a great cancer-fighting agent. It attacks certain bile acids reducing their toxicity. It is both a soluble and insoluble fiber. Soluble fiber may reduce the bad cholesterol without lowering the good cholesterol. It is also found that those who eat more oats are less likely to develop heart disease. Oatmeal is a good source of many nutrients including vitamin E, zinc, selenium, copper, iron, and magnesium. How can you continue to hate something with all these benefits for a healthy life?

You must find a new name and a new way to enjoy the things you hate. My new name for oatmeal is granola! I love granola.

Just like my bad introduction to oatmeal, the way you are introduced to sex weighs a lot on your view of it today.

A few years ago, I had to explain sex to my three girls ages eight, nine, and eleven. Several of their cousins were having babies, out of wedlock, and my girls just didn't understand how this could happen. After trying to give my girls a G-rated version of sex, they didn't get it. My eleven year old, ReNay, had even read a series of books that introduced sex at age-appropriate intervals. So, finally, I said to my girls, "Do you really want to know?" and we began a long discussion about sex.

Once you understand the conception for sex, you begin to embark on its intention.

At the end of our talk, my girls were saying things like "I will NEVER do that" and "Yuck! How disgusting!" I had to continue to talk with them explaining God's creation of this intimacy that should only be between a loving husband and wife. I also shared with them that their existence was formed by God during an intimate time with Mommy and Daddy. They had many questions and are even still approaching me with additional questions.

If your first introduction to sex was presented with a biblical prospective, you see sex as sanctified. You see it as a gift from God. In his book, *The Cross-Centered Life*, C.

J. Malhaney says 'sanctification is a process. It is the process of becoming more like Christ—of growing in holiness'. If you view sex as a process of becoming more like Christ and growing in holiness, your introduction had to be one where sex was selfless. But this process of seeing sex as sanctified has to begin with throwing out the distorted views that cause you to bristle when your husband approaches you.

If your first introduction to sex made you feel like it was dirty or not desirable, you saw sex in a sinful light. If I had stopped with only what the sex act looks like with my girls, they would be stuck to form their own opinion about sexual intimacy. You, like my girls, must be freed from that image of sex being dirty and transform that view to God's truth regarding sex. If no transformation takes place, then somewhere in your mind you will always see sex as sin. No matter your husband's approach, sex will be tainted to you until you are set free by the truth.

Have you ever wondered (or even asked) where your husband got his first knowledge and understanding of sexual intimacy?

In order to change how you accept or reject his advances, you must change your mind about why sex was created in the first place. Once you understand the conception for sex, you begin to embark on its intention. Knowing the purpose of something's creation will help you understand its intention for existing.

Because of his God-given sex drive, a husband can look at his wife and feel a desire to be intimate with her. But does he understand why he has a sex drive in the first place? In Joshua Harris's book, *Sex Is Not the Problem (Lust Is)*, he says that God gives us our drives so we would drive toward something...being a sexual being with sexual drives is part of what it means to be a human created in God's image.

What is your husband driving towards? His sex drive should drive him toward intimacy with you and God. Yes, sex should drive us toward sanctification.

How Is Sex Sanctified?

In the area of sex, so many of us have gotten so much wrong information that we cannot see the holiness of sexual intimacy without the tainted view of sin. I need you to understand what sanctification really is so I am giving you the definition.

sanc·ti·fy

1. To set apart for sacred use; consecrate.

2. To free somebody from sin: to perform a ritual or other act intended to free somebody from sin.

God desired a relationship with man so He created him and set man apart for sacred use. He placed him in a beautiful garden, provided him with gainful employment, and gave him all that he desired to eat. God gave to man never expecting man to pay Him back. God desired man to love Him and worship Him and (be grateful) for all that He chose to lavish on him, and man believed.

Soon man chose to listen to the Father of Lies who deceived him out of all that God had given to him and put a gulf between God and man. But Romans 5:8 says, "God shows his love for us in that while we were still sinners, Christ died for us." God had mercy and decided to send His only Son as a tangible reminder of His love and all that He has in store for us.

Jesus chose to obey His Father. He came to show the intimate relationship between Father and Son so that sons of man (you and I) might be redeemed and restored back to a perfect relationship with God through Jesus' death on the cross. He gave his life so we might see a picture of God's love for us.

At the age of twenty-one, I accepted Christ as my Savior. Everything seemed different. I was excited about life and couldn't wait to learn more about God. My entire outlook on life changed. I believed on the Lord Jesus Christ and I was saved from the penalty of sin.

When you accept Jesus as your personal Savior and Lord, you get the gift of abundant life. The relationship that you have with Christ allows you to view life through new eyes. It grants you the ability to see life with God's hand woven through it. Even when someone you love dies, you are able to see eternal life as the reward. Death means life for those who believe (Philippians 1:21).

But the deceiver continues to lie about all that God has given to us through His Son's death on the cross. When Christians listen to Satan's lies, they walk in a distortion of the truth. They live life without the abundant blessing of God; they live with a partial image of truth that God has created sex and set it apart for sacred use. Sex is sanctified and sanctioned by God.

Sanctification of Sex and Satan's Distortion of It

God had mercy and decided to send a picture of His love to His people through a healthy marital relationship right in each home of His believers. God placed a mom and a dad in the home for the children to see God's love for His Bride, the church. He knew we needed to have safety and security as a daily reminder of His love for us. God also wants your children to visibly see a picture, through mom and dad's relationship, of how much He loves them. He wanted our kids to have a daily picture to know the love that is in store for them.

But the Devil is still tricking us out of this intimate relationship in the home. Most husbands and wives are living without safety and security in their homes. This safety and security is defunct because marital intimacy is dysfunctional. And if this describes your home, your children are living with a messed-up image of God.

God set this husband-wife relationship apart and the sexual intimacy between couples is sacred. Sex is a picture of the holiness of God in a marriage. It is set apart for sacred use.

Satan continues to lie and allows us to believe that sex is not set apart for sacred use. He tells us that sex is free to give and take to whomever we desire. Because we don't flee and match up Satan's lies to God's Word, so many of us are not seeing the sanctification of sexual intimacy. You need to see sex as sacred. You need to see sex as sanctified. Sex is there to make you holy, and to free you from the sin of the tainted view of intimacy. It is the process of becoming more like Christ in your marriage. Ephesians 5:31-32 says, "Therefore a man shall leave his father and mother and hold fast to his wife, and the two shall become one flesh."

God's intimacy with man is shown in His love and provision for him. God acted and displayed His love to us by sending his Son. Your intimacy with Christ should be shown in the attitude and love you have for your spouse, children and others. Your relationship with Christ should be evident to your family and friends.

Your intimacy with your husband is displayed in the way you respond to him, and your children are the benefactors of this relationship. Your intimacy with your husband provides safety and security to you and your children. In 2004, at the Desiring God National Conference, John Piper gave a series of lessons entitled, "Sex and the Supremacy of Christ." Pastor Piper made two simple points:

> 1. All sexual corruption serves to conceal the true knowledge of Christ, but

> 2. The true knowledge of Christ serves to prevent sexual corruption.

The deceiver has tricked us into believing that all that God has bestowed on us isn't all that there is. He wants this sexual corruption, all around us, to conceal the true knowledge of Christ. He wants to keep us bound by the lies and distortion he has created in our intimacy. He wants us to believe that God is holding out on us. So he has placed a huge gulf in the middle of our relationship, and now we have become sick of sex, thinking this is not all there could possibly be. We have been tricked to remove the picture of holiness from our sexual intimacy.

Every time you are intimate with your husband, it should serve as a reminder that God desires to be intimately close to you. During the intimate act of sex, you and your husband appear to be inseparable. This act is so close, so entangling, that two people appear to be one. This is the same with our intimate relationship with Christ. You are His bride, the church. Your intimacy with Christ is the process of becoming one with Him.

But Satan not only has us doubting God, he has us doubting our husbands. We doubt that he has right intentions or motives. He has us doubting whether we even need a husband or not. The enemy is saying to us, "Why can't this relationship be shown without you having to deal with the sexual stuff?" Or, better yet, "why do you even need him in the home?" Even better still, "why can't this relationship be shown better between two men or two women? Wouldn't it make more sense to have this relationship between two people that already communicate alike and are similar?" (God says in Leviticus 18:22, "you shall not lie with a male as with a woman, it is an abomination.") Satan says to us, "As long as there is love, relationships do not have to be displayed exactly as God says. God only told you half of the truth. Relationships can be perfect and lovingly displayed as long as you are happy." Lies. Lies. Lies!

Satan continues his lies and we take heed to it. Because this sexual relationship takes work and causes us pain, we believe that pain cannot be part of God's plan. The world, the flesh, and the devil continue to tell us that as long as it feels good, do it. God never intended for you to be completely happy and free of pain. Happiness is a temporary state. Anyone who is always happy is not living in reality. Happiness is threatened, daily, by death, illness, circumstances, and sin (and many other things). Have you ever heard someone say, "I am so happy to have pneumonia? I needed this rest!" No! Happiness is just one of the many feelings experienced in a well-rounded life.

There are reasons you can enjoy the happy state. You are grateful for it because you know what the unhappy state looks like. In order to truly grasp the joy of happiness, you have to have walked through something unhappy, either yourself or someone you love. True happiness is appreciated more by those who have reason to appreciate the happiness. But happiness is not the feeling we should strive for. Living life with all different emotions will catapult you towards contentment.

During our seminary days of poverty, we appreciated and were grateful for the times of excess. For many of us, we are grateful for God's provision when we have walked through some very lean times.

When you experience childbirth, when you are in the middle of the pains you could have easily screamed out: "Take me home, Lord Jesus!" But as soon as the baby is delivered, you see all that you have to live for.

God has set sex apart for the pleasure of marriage. Sex takes work, maintenance, and obedience, and sex is only sanctified between a man and a woman who have committed to being married for a lifetime and desire to bring glory to God.

> Sanctified sex is selfless.
> Sanctified sex is serving.
> Sanctified sex is glorified sex. Supernaturally made superior.
> Sanctified sex brings pleasure to God.

In Revelations 4:11, John writes, "Thou are worthy, O Lord, to receive glory and honour and power: for thou hast created all things, and for thy pleasure they are and were created" (KJV). When we are a part of anything that brings glory to God, it not only brings pleasure to God but it also brings pleasure to us. Being a part of anything that you know is bringing glory to God, no matter how difficult, brings you to a place of contentment.

Sanctified Sex Changes Your Heart

You may not be able to go back to your first introduction of sex and get a proper perspective. What you can do is understand and be thankful for the creation of sex and change your view to appreciate this unique and special intimate relationship.

If we truly were experiencing all that sex was created to be, we would forget about the kids and live in the bedroom. (That eight-month old would have to get his own breakfast.) We would forget about our jobs and wake to enjoy sex. (Who needs money anyways? We could live on love.) There would be no need for food, because this sanctified sex would be enough to sustain you. (Why not die poor and hungry but sexually satisfied?)

Unrealistic as this sounds, a clear view of why God created sex and that it is set apart for marriage, is what will drive you to intimacy. Seeing the sanctification in sex will drive your intimacy with your husband and renew your intimacy with God. You will desire to glorify God in your sexual relationship. You will see the need for God's boundaries, and why sex is held in high-esteem by God.

God set sex apart for marriage. But sex in marriage can still be sin (we will cover this in Sin of Sex chapter). To have sanctified sex, it has to come from a pure heart—a heart committed to doing the will of God, not full of lust or shame.

I grew up in a Holiness Church and when anyone came to accept Jesus as Savior, the church would say, "the devil's lost another soul." That is correct. The day you surrendered your life to Christ, you were set apart for sacred use. Satan, realizing his loss, decided to wage war against you. He knew he could not do one thing about your new permanent status in Heaven so he determined to keep you so preoccupied that your sacred use would be hindered and limited.

The enemy knows we now know the truth about him and his ways. He goes after what is most sacred to us. He wants our family, our legacy, so he begins at the core—our personal intimacy with our husbands. And we have been deeply injured by this attack on our marriages. But do we know how to live in light of this newfound truth?

> You: Lord, I believe everything You have told me. But how do I live it out?

> God: In Psalm 40:1: "I waited patiently for the Lord; He inclined to me and heard my cry."

> You: But Lord, I'm tired. It's too hard. I don't have the strength or energy.

> God: Isaiah 40:31: "but they who wait for the Lord shall renew their strength; they shall mount up with wings like eagles; they shall run and not be weary; they shall walk and not faint."

> You: Lord, I really don't think I can. I have seen you do so much in so many

areas, but I feel beat in this one. Are you able to fix this one?

God: Proverbs 3:5-6: "Trust in the Lord with all your heart, and do not lean on your own understanding. In all your ways acknowledge Him, and He will make straight your paths." And Jeremiah 32:17: "Ah, Sovereign Lord, you have made the Heavens and the earth by your great power and outstretched arm. Nothing is too hard for you."

You: Lord, I'm scared. Will you be there every step of this journey?

God: Hebrews 3:5-6: "I will never leave you nor forsake you."

We can confidently say, "The Lord is my helper; I will not fear; what can man do to me?"(Heb. 13:6). We need to ask God to purge the entire untruth that has been etched in our minds. Even though our introduction to intimacy was marred, there is absolutely nothing too difficult for our God to transform.

In 1 Thessalonians 4:3-4, it says, "for this is the will of God, your sanctification: that you abstain from sexual immorality; that each one of you know how to control his own body in holiness and honor." God has set you apart for a sacred purpose. You are sanctified in Christ. God has set sexual intimacy apart for a sacred purpose in marriage. Your sexual intimacy with your husband is sanctified in Christ. To see sex any other way is sin and we need to get the sin out of our sex.

Yes, many of us did not receive a sanctified version of sex when we were first introduced to it. So we must create an occasion where we re-introduce sex, God's way. We will need to find a new name for sexual intimacy with our husbands, so we can have a fresh prospective on a subject that initially was tainted for us.

Tonight, you need to say to your husband, "I have a special piece of chocolate cake waiting for you in the bedroom." (If you were born another shade like vanilla, use vanilla cake or coconut crème pie.) After the kids are in bed, you take your husband to the bedroom and share with him this new dessert that you have set apart for him. You can watch the smirk on his face when he visits a friend's house and is offered a serving of chocolate cake or crème pie.

> For God has not called us for impurity, but
> in holiness — (1 Thessalonians 4:7)

JOURVOTIONAL

Sanctification or Sin?

1. What was the first time you can remember hearing and understanding the word sex?

_____

_____

_____

2. Think of some of the things you detested but now see as a vital for your health (ex. vitamins, exercise). Write some here.

_____

_____

_____

_____

3. Do you view sex as sanctified, set apart as sacred, or in a sinful light, something to hide? Why?

_____

_____

_____

_____

4. Where did your husband get his first knowledge and understanding of sexual intimacy?

_____

_____

_____

5. Write these words in your own penmanship: *Sex is set apart for sacred use (sanctified) and sanctioned (approved) by God.*

_____

_____

Do you really believe the above statement? Why or why not?

_____

_____

_____

6. With sex all around us, we may not be able to remember our first introduction. After reading this chapter, what are some things that you believe God wants you to know about sexual intimacy that you have never noted before?

_____

_____

_____

7. Put the date that you came to know Christ as Savior if you remember. _____ That is the date war was waged against you.

What was the date you and your husband were married? _____ That is the date war was waged against your marriage.

8. Read again these scriptures from the above chapter: Psalm 40:1, Isaiah 40:31, Proverbs 3:5-6, Jeremiah 32:17, and Hebrews 3:5-6. What is God specifically telling you about your intimacy with your husband?

_____

_____

_____

_____

9. If sexual intimacy has a tinge of sin tied to it for you, you need a new name for sex. What is your new name for intimacy?

_____

_____

_____

S.O.S. — CHAPTER #9

SENSITIZE OUR SPOUSE

Husbands, love your wives, and be not bitter against them. — (Colossians 3:19)

In the McKelvy household, we have created a family full of music lovers. Recently, I woke up in the middle of the night and was horrified by a CD that had become a family favorite. It has some of the best singing we had ever heard, but the content was something we would never have picked for our children to hear. But by this time, even our two year old could sing all the words to these songs. One woman was begging her lover not to throw her away, she was "not leaving. You're the best man I'll ever know." Another woman was leaving her husband because "He won't listen." Ray said we were "lovers of good music but went digging through the trash can to find it."

There are many reasons that our sexual relationship is in the trashcan. Many women would agree that the primary reason is their husbands. Men are just not sensitive, and if they would just be more sensitive, our sexual relationship would flourish. Sexual intimacy is a form of communication, and if this man knew how to love and cherish me, we would be in a totally different spot than we are now.

We believe our husbands' insensitivity has caused us to become sick of sex, and if he would change, then our sex life and marriage would change. But if we are honest, the sensitivity in both our communication styles was poor long before our intimacy began deteriorating.

146

In order to sensitize our spouses, we must be willing to remember why God created us in the first place. He made us a helper. Now, we have been a capable helper in most areas. We work full time jobs to help out with the finances. We are efficient helpers in our homes—they run pretty smoothly because of our effort to keep order. But God made us a helper in every aspect of the relationship. We are a helper to our husband even in his communication.

Sex is a very important form of communication in marriage. If you and your husband are not communicating effectively in your sexual intimacy, you have fallen down on your job as a helper.

Sexual intimacy reflects how we are communicating with each other. His desire to have sex with you when communication is lacking is because of his makeup. Sex is his way of wanting to reconnect with you. Most men would agree that sex would get boring, even to them, without the relationship with their wives.

Men are generally task oriented. Once they are finished with whatever they are working on or talking about, they move on to the next thing. If you begin an argument with him and stop talking, he feels like the argument and all that goes with it, is complete. He is now on to the next thing.

Because he has this God-given desire to be with you physically, his sex drive, he thinks that is the next thing and moves to let you know how much he desires you. The only thing is, he has forgotten to add your feelings into the equation. This is where you come in. Our husbands need us to help them understand our makeup: How we feel about one area of our lives affects everything. Our feelings are so much a part of who we are.

If your husband is not adding your feelings to intimacy, then you are both allowing him to treat you as a fellow male. Men have a tendency to do things whether it feels right or not. They are doers. You must help your spouse become sensitive to you. You are not here to change who he is as a man, only to help him respond to you and have a perpetual sensitivity to you as a woman.

Once your spouse shows sensitivity to you sexually, it creates a whole new view of sex for you. But most of us have failed to help our spouses understand the need for his sensitivity—not just in the sexual area, but in every area.

I always thought Ray should just *know* some things. I mean, do I have to tell him everything? Yes! Men and women are innately different. You have to tell him so he knows. You have to tell him more than once if he doesn't get it, and you have to continually tell him until he understands.

He needs you to help him learn what sensitivity looks like to you and sensitivity will look different to every woman. Depending on your unique makeup, you sensitivity needs will look completely different than mine. Your husband only needs to understand one woman's unique sensitivity needs—yours. You are the only one who can help him understand your uniqueness.

If you are new on a job, usually there is someone available to train you. She sits beside you to help you when you need help. It is great to have her close at hand. Once you are comfortable with your job, even when a situation comes up that you've never seen before (or have forgotten how to do), she is available.

Likewise, you are your husband's sensitivity trainer. Once he has the skills, so carefully taught by you, he can deliver them to you. And when he forgets how to manage "your unique sensitivity needs," you are there to add encouragement and instruction. No one is defensive with their trainer but instead looks to him or her for help.

I need Ray to understand what sensitivity looks like to me. I am the only one who can help him understand what my needs look like. No one else can tell him; I am, after all, God's chosen helper for Ray. Likewise, you are the only one who can show your husband what your unique needs are.

Communicating the Day-to-day Stuff

How do you tell your husband that you received a call from the phone company saying that your payment is overdue? If you approach him in love as an oversight, he will hear you. If you approach him with disgust over his inabilities, he will shut down.

The way you establish communication about the day-to-day stuff will affect how you communicate with your husband sexually. Even more important, the way he hears you communicate the day-to-day stuff will either keep his ear tuned in to you or tuned out. Your husband will learn to respond to you in the way he has learned to hear the majority of what you are saying to him. Honestly, you will talk about the day-to-day stuff more often than you will talk about sex.

With nine kids, I have learned to hear my kids and respond based on what I hear. I can tell if the cry is real or put on. I can tell if the cry is because of pain or if it is a cry because of hurt feelings. I have learned to respond to each of my kids based on what I hear them saying to me, whether they are literally talking or not.

When what my kids are saying doesn't seem important, it doesn't get an immediate reaction from me. If someone is crying a big, loud cry because someone hurt their feelings, I may not come right away. They may even think I am ignoring them. But let one of them let out a yell that registers pain, and I am running to see what is going on. I want to alleviate their pain. I want to be there to hear what happened.

Your husband needs you to speak to him in tones, language, and love so that he doesn't ignore what you are saying. He needs to be able to hear you even when you are not speaking. But when you are speaking, he needs to *want* to hear what you are telling him. His desire to want to hear what you are saying primarily starts with you.

Communicating the day-to-day stuff requires that you "speak the truth in love" (Ephesians 4:15). This conversation is free from pretense, simulation, falsehood, accusations, and deceit. They are kind words that "minister grace to the hearer" (Ephesians 4:29). This kind of conversation makes the listener want to hear the speaker and want to hear more of what is being said.

> *How much* do you want him to hear?
> *What* do you want him to hear?
> *Are you willing to learn* to communicate with him so he will hear?

Is He Really Hearing How I Feel?

In order for your husband to really hear how you feel, you once again, must be who God created you to be: his helper.

There is a slight problem with being helper. We must know when our husbands need help. Many of us have fallen prey to the curse and have forsaken the "helper"

151

title and have moved to the "rule over" title. We have taken over.

In Genesis 3:1-6, it says, "Now the serpent was more crafty than any of the wild animals the Lord God had made. He said to the woman, "Did God really say, 'You must not eat from any tree in the garden'?" The woman said to the serpent, "We may eat fruit from the trees in the garden, but God did say, 'You must not eat fruit from the tree that is in the middle of the garden, and you must not touch it, or you will die.' " "You will not surely die," the serpent said to the woman. "For God knows that when you eat of it your eyes will be opened, and you will be like God, knowing good and evil." When the woman saw that the fruit of the tree was good for food and pleasing to the eye, and also desirable for gaining wisdom, she took some and ate it. She also gave some to her husband, who was with her, and he ate it."

Here we actually see the biblical story of the fall of man. God chooses to tell us that the serpent was craftier than any other animal. When Satan determines to launch his attack against the family, he knows who to talk to. In my mind, I am sure when the serpent eavesdropped on Adam and Eve's conversations he could see that Eve was the faster, more emotional, and the more outspoken talker of the two. Even when Eve had an opportunity to ask Adam for clarification of what the serpent told her

God has said, she just went ahead and answered for the both of them.

When our daughter, Ravin, was about five years old, she asked her daddy for potato chips as I was preparing dinner. When I overheard her request, I interrupted and told her, "No chips before dinner." She politely and as firmly as a five-year-old could, said to me, "Mommy, I am talking to Daddy!" After the initial shock of this child calling me out, I realized she was right. I began looking to see how many other times I had stolen Ray's voice from him in our home. And there were many. My husband does have to have a voice in our home.

A husband's own voice gives him the safety to say what is on his mind. Knowing that he can express what is going on in his own heart will allow him the ability to hear what is going on in yours. No one wants to listen if they never get an opportunity to speak.

When your husband was a child, he learned to listen and respond based on his parents' voices and tone. He is no longer a part of his original biological household, but his tendency is to continue to hear the way he has always known. It is how he has been trained to hear, but he is not stuck. He can learn to respond to you and hear how you feel if you are willing to help him hear you.

If you respond to your husband in a way that is tolerable to him, he will want to hear and to please you. Soon, he will begin to ask you questions about how something made you feel. It's true! He will begin to hear and respond to you—asking questions until he understands where you are coming from. I believe every husband who desires to walk and be obedient to God desires to please his wife. He just needs you to talk to him like God talks to him—in a way he can hear you.

Sensitivity is relative. Everyone has a different need of sensitivity. Your level is different than mine, so you have to become the sensitivity teacher to your own husband. Many of us do not know what we really need in regards to sensitivity. We just know when our level of sensitivity is not being met. Having a super-sensitive guy who shows his love in icky, sticky, mushy ways would have to have a wife that thinks icky, sticky, and mushy is heaven.

Everyone has a different need of sensitivity.

To another, anything sticky would need to be cleaned up with hot water and thrown out with the garbage.

What makes your sensitivity meter register? Communicate in a way your husband can hear, and you will have the most sensitive man the world has to offer—to you.

To sensitize our spouses, we have to realize the level of sensitivity he portrays to you is the level of sensitivity you have taught him that you need. It is time for us to pull ourselves up by the bootstraps and tackle this task of becoming an effective sensitivity teacher to our own husbands. To have a sensitive spouse, there must be an

154

atmosphere where he can walk through the door and hear what you want him to hear and respond with your unique needs in mind.

This will not happen without a valiant effort from you believing this is God's unique gift to you and He has made the perfect choice in your husband. So God will walk beside you, daily, as you gently teach your husband what sensitivity looks like to you.

> *So, that we may no longer be children, tossed to and fro by the waves and carried about by every wind of doctrine, by human cunning, by craftiness in deceitful schemes. Rather, speaking the truth in love, we are to grow up in every way into him who is the head, into Christ.* —(Ephesians 4:14-15)

JOURVOTIONAL

Sensitize Our Spouse

1. What characteristics would the ideal sensitive man have?

_____

_____

2. Looking at your list, would you say your husband displays some or most of these qualities? Which ones?

_____

_____

_____

_____

3. What are some things your husband could do to show his sensitivity towards you?

_____

_____

_____

_____

4. Have you communicated these desires to him? _____
If so, specifically how and when?

_____

_____

_____

5. How do you communicate the day-to-day stuff?

_____

_____

_____

6. How do you communicate your sensitivity needs to your husband?

_____

_____

_____

7. Compare the answers from numbers 5 and 6 above and write out differences, if any.

_____

_____

_____

_____

8. Is there an area in your marriage where you have gone from being a helper for your husband to ruling over him?

_____

_____

9. Ask a dear friend to be totally honest and tell you if she sees an area in your life where you are ruling over your husband and write her response here.

_____

_____

_____

_____

10. Looking at your husband, list some ways you see his sensitivity played out.

_____

_____

_____

11. Read Ephesians 4:14-15. Why is speaking the truth so important?

_____

_____

_____

Ways to Begin to Sensitize Your Husbands

1. Tape record yourself or stop and rethink the way you expressed your last message or instruction to your husband. The next time, try to express it a different way, in a different tone. (Maybe sing the instruction or message, to add a dance to it while you are saying it, zazz hands, a high five, etc.— something different and memorable)

2. Memorize Philippians 4:6-7.

S.O.S. — CHAPTER #10

SHARE OUR STORIES: JANET

"For a marriage relationship to flourish, there must be intimacy. It takes an enormous amount of courage to say to your spouse, 'This is me. I'm not proud of it — in fact, I'm a little embarrassed by it — but this is who I am.'" — Bill Hybels

The book of Hosea isn't a popular book in the Bible. We don't often hear preachers preach from it quite as often as Philippians, Romans, or Hebrews. It is hard for me to hear the story of Hosea because he was asked by God to chase an unfaithful wife. Hosea's wife was a prostitute named Gomer. Her name means completion.

My name is Janet. I am a living, breathing replica of Gomer and divinely, my name means "God's grace." I am able to see God's grace every day of my life as I live with the Gomer in me.

My mother was married with two children when she divorced her unfaithful alcoholic husband. After marrying my dad, I was the only child born to this union. Their marriage was filled with fighting. I would hide in a space between the counter and refrigerator hearing Dad's laughter as mom, in her anger, would hurl glasses at him. It was no laughing matter when mom arrived home from work one night to find my dad sodomizing my brother. They divorced when I was four. My mom kept that secret for years and I didn't understand what my sister and brother meant when they called me "the pervert's kid."

I still visited my father every other weekend and he never touched me sexually. Each birthday or Christmas, until I was ten, the perfect gift would have been for my parents to reunite. I blamed myself for the split.

We moved in with my grandparents for a while until my mother married again. This kind man provided for us as if we were his own. Living in two households, I had no clear boundaries. I didn't have many friends; I was the outcast and unaccepted one. There were two basic reasons, (1) I told so many lies and (2) I was from the "divorced" family.

At twelve, I was introduced to sex. I knew this activity was wrong and I felt dirty and ashamed. No one told me but I knew it had to be a secret. I had one friend. She was also outcast and living with her single mom. At her home, there were always pornographic books and we began reading them together.

My real dad moved to another city when I was thirteen and I lost my special spot with my step-dad. After eight years of marriage and believing he couldn't have children, my baby sister was born. He began yelling at us and doting on this "golden" child. Not having my own father around left an empty spot in my life. With my dad now in another city, the restraining force in my life was gone. His presence kept me from going wild and with him gone, wild I went.

When I was fourteen, I chose a guy at school and told him, "I don't want to be a virgin anymore and I want you to be the first one." I felt like I had a whore's heart from the beginning.

That same year, I accidentally overdosed. Drugs were easily assessable because my brother sold them out of our home, unbeknownst to my mother. The hospital made me see a psychiatrist and at one session, I found out what happened when my parents divorced.

I began seeking sex as a way of having people like me. I wanted to be popular. I gained popularity, all right, as the school slut. I began to hate school and smoke pot to get through it.

For my fifteenth birthday, my brother gave me my first hit of acid. Speed later became my drug of choice. Soon,

I skipped a lot of school and began dealing drugs to support my own habit. I was living in a drug house with five others by the age of seventeen. But a vice principal saw my potential and had me enter a program to finish my high school education.

Sex, drugs, and rock 'n' roll was the meaning of life to me. It wasn't a glamorous life. I worked a minimum wage job but eventually became a bar tender for cash to support my habit. My habit cost me more than you can image. I never stayed in one place too long, and my promiscuous lifestyle meant birth control pills or drugs. Every time the choice came up, I'd choose drugs.

At twenty-one I became pregnant and I knew with the lifestyle I was living, a baby was out of the question. My catholic boyfriend was totally against abortion but to me there was no other option. For three weeks following the procedure, I was flooded with depression. Planned Parenthood may tell you differently, but I knew I had murdered. I killed my baby.

After that break-up, I dated my new boyfriend for five years off and on. He was twelve years older than me but I could not be faithful to him. I was set into a pattern of rebellion. I had no self-respect, no self-worth, and no self-esteem. At this point, if anyone approached me sexually, I couldn't say "no." The Gomer in me drew me sexually to men. I felt like I needed sex.

My second pregnancy with my older boyfriend ended in miscarriage. Coming home one day, I found my boyfriend in bed with another woman. To me it justified me ending my third pregnancy with another abortion.

Money was really tight at this period in my life. When I found out I was pregnant a fourth time, I didn't have the $250.00 for the abortion. I saved the money but because I waited so long, I had to have the two-day procedure. But God's grace still covered me.

When I was twenty-five, I left a party at midnight. Driving 55 miles an hour, I ran head-on into a cement median. I lay in the ditch, in shock, and bleeding internally until 4:30 a.m. On the way home from his night shift at the hospital, a paramedic found me. My spleen was ruptured and I had a broken femur. The doctor told my parents not to expect me to live.

At the hospital, my sister whispered to me over and over again, "God saved you for a reason." I stayed in the hospital for a month and then with my sister for six additional recovery weeks. I began going to bars and dove back into my old lifestyle with renewed vigor. More sex, more drugs, and more drug dealing.

Because of my continued falling asleep on the job, a drug test was ordered. My positive drug test meant I was fired. By God's grace, only a week later, I landed a job through a temporary agency at a Bank. It was my first white-collared job and I didn't want to screw it up. I would call in sick if I didn't have drugs to get through the day. But the drugs left me empty inside and I was searching for another high.

I tried many churches but it was futile. I wasn't sure if I was "good enough" to make it to Heaven and I wasn't sure if I was destined for Hell. So I plunged into Astrology. In it I found just enough truth but so many let downs.

At work, one day, I overheard two co-workers talking. I wasn't intentionally eavesdropping but the conversation peaked my interest. They were discussing the difference between religion versus relationship. One of the employees' names was Janice, everyone called her "Jan." Her name, like mine means, "God's grace."

In November, the bank hired me at a salary. It was the best job I'd ever had even though I kept my job bartending to support my habit.

Jan worked for the bank's mortgage broker. The bank was small so we were all friends. At lunch, I shared with Jan some of what was going on in my life and she responded, "That is how I felt before I accepted Christ." I had sought out religion many times but these words haunted me. One day, I hunted Jan down to ask her, "What's this accepting Christ thing?" and she invited me to her church.

I was too hung over and tired to make it that Sunday, but I visited the next week. Jan never told me her husband was the preacher. But it was the first time I felt like God's Word was applicable. My bartending shift that day was from 1:00 p.m. to 1:00 a.m. I couldn't shake the sermon and I began telling customers about the church.

Jan invited me to a Bible study at her home that Tuesday evening. Not one of the four normal attendees came and she shared "Steps to peace with God" with me. This small Campus Crusade for Christ tract was the answer. It was the answer to all I was looking for in drugs and alcohol. I gave up drugs that very evening and have not had any to this day.

By God's grace, my car broke down soon thereafter. On Wednesdays and Sundays, Jan and her husband would take me to their home, feed me, and go to church. I was starved for a new life and I ate up this time with them.

Jan soon began to meet with me weekly and take me through a study called, "10 Steps to Christian Maturity." Three weeks into this study, I quit working at the bar. That Christmas, my offering to Jesus was to quit smoking. In January, my roommate moved out because she said, "You are not the same Janet I moved in with."

When I became a Christian, I desired to serve Christ with the same vigor I had served Satan. I still didn't have a car so I began riding the bus. I shared Christ with everyone on the bus and my pastor said of me, "This is a whole new meaning to bus ministry."

My family could see all the changes but weren't sure what I was into now. My new life verse was Psalm 40:1-3, "I waited patiently for the Lord; he inclined to me and heard my cry. He drew me up from the pit of destruction, out of the miry bog, and set my feet upon a rock, making my steps secure. He put a new song in my mouth, a song of praise to our God. Many will see and fear, and put their trust in the Lord." There were so many changes in my life, inside and out. So, when my dad died in June, I was so thankful that he could die proud of me—proud I was no longer on drugs, proud I was in a stable job, proud of the change in my heart.

I had such a hunger for God that with my inheritance money, I paid off my debts and went to Calvary Bible College. When the money ran out, I began working for the phone company. There, I met Sam.

Sam was a Christian man. He was kind and compassionate. But even with my new faith, the draw for sex was strong. Even as Christians, we kept finding ourselves sexually involved. So we married. Most don't see this as a good reason to marry, but we wanted to be obedient to the Word so we followed 1 Corinthians 7:9 and married rather than to burn with passion and continue in sin.

I had such fantasies about how marriage and sexual intimacy would be. I had to make many adjustments because I soon found that sex was not going to measure up to my fantasies. But God has given me satisfaction, sexually, with my husband.

Of course, sex isn't all that there is. For years I felt as if I married the wrong guy. I was constantly battling being forgiven. I knew I was a murderer. But one friend assured me: "Paul murdered Christians. God forgives every sin and delights in the forgiven."

Then Sam made some unwise choices that affected our entire family. So one Sunday evening I had had it. I packed myself, the kids, and the car. He had gone out and I was moving out that very evening.

Trying to gather my thoughts, I stopped by a small Bible church in my neighborhood for their Sunday Evening service. I placed both children in childcare and settled in the church for "Anything, Lord."

The second song was God's voice to me. This simple song by Don Moen says:

> "God will make a way
> Where there seems to be no way
> He works in ways we cannot see
> He will make a way for me.
> He will be my guide
> Hold me closely to His side
> With love and strength for each new day
> He will make a way. He will make a way."

That night, I knew the Holy Spirit was telling me to "Go Home." And I knew I was supposed to do for Sam what God had done for me many times before. (Show him grace.) This is exactly what God has given me the strength to do. If it had been left up to me, I would have walked out a thousand times. But, my name means God's grace. The Gomer in me is transformed. I am a daily administer of God's grace. My name is Janet.

***

Janet is one of the most prayerful people I know. Looking from the outside in, you may think she and Sam are spiritually mismatched. Looking from the outside in, you may see a struggling family. Looking from the outside in, you may see continuous relationship issues. But, when you see Janet's heart displayed from the inside out, you see a woman of grace. You see a woman in the midst of a journey with God that is not easy, convenient, or fun. In Janet's words on her life, "I wouldn't have been as happy, learned as much, or grown as much spiritually" if her situation was different and "I definitely wouldn't be the woman of prayer I am today."

JOURVOTIONAL

Share Our Stories: Janet

1. What does your name mean?

_____

2. Divorce is devastating to children, yet it is all around us. List ten people you know that have experienced the pain of divorce.

_____

_____

_____

_____

3. Among your friends and family members, whom do you know where children are living between two different homes?

_____

_____

4. Sexual abuse is rampant in our country. Write the initials of five or more people you know who have experienced the pain of sexual abuse.

_____

_____

_____

5. When was the first time you understand a difference between religion and relationship?

_____

_____

6. Abortion and miscarriage are devastating to any mother. Who is the first person you think of when you hear those words?

_____

7. What do you think God's purpose is for having you here on Earth?

_____

_____

_____

_____

_____

_____

8. Can you name a person who has been a person of grace to you?

_____

9. Name a person who has invested in your spiritual life.

_____

10. No marriage is perfect. Name some ways you have been a minister of grace to your husband.

_____

_____

_____

11. Read again Psalm 40:1-3, and fill in the blanks:

> I waited patiently (when _____)
> for the Lord; he inclined to me and heard
> my cry (what were you crying for _____).
> He drew me up from the pit of destruc-
> tion, out of the miry bog, and set my feet
> upon a rock, making my steps secure
> (specifically how _____).
> He put a new song in my mouth (what is
> the song or transformation _____)
> a song of praise to our God. May will see
> and fear (list some who watched you walk
> through this time _____),
> and put their trust in the Lord.

S.O.S. — CHAPTER #11

SICK OF SPOUSE

*It is better to dwell in the wilderness, than
with a contentious and angry woman.*
— (Proverbs 21:19)

You may have reason to blame your spouse for you feeling sick of sex and every other ailment you have. He has caused you many headaches and now these headaches have become so severe that they cause nausea. He is kind of like a constant migraine, and you cannot wait to alleviate the pain. There have been years of disappointment, expectations not met, and you have nothing to talk about anymore. You have a lot of issues with him, and frankly, you feel like it would be easier to get rid of him than to try to work it out. In some way, I completely understand your pain.

A few years ago, we were looking to adopt. We heard of a little girl named Rose and she soon came to live with us. My husband and children were extremely happy because they had been praying for this new addition to our home for a long time. I, on the other hand, wasn't quite so sure. Being the stay-at-home mother of eight, at this time, I knew most of the responsibility for caring for her would fall on my shoulders, but we knew she needed a place to live. So we paid the astronomical adoption fees for her to become a part of our family.

Rose was absolutely adorable at first and because she was so young, I knew it would probably be easy for her to graft into our home. But, because of her background and her family of origin, there were constant battles. I ended up hating the fact that she was a part of our family.

Rose made messes all the time and never cleaned up after herself. She would turn up her nose at the food we bought and constantly pilfered through the trashcan. We disciplined her over and over for the things that would cause her harm; yet she continually did them. So after a while, she stopped doing them in our presence; just behind our backs, hoping we wouldn't find out. We found out every time because she was incapable of thoroughly cleaning up after herself.

One day, we all entered the house through the garage while Rose stayed outside to play. Soon, we found out that she had run away. We did all that we were supposed to do to find her. We called the proper authorities in runaway cases like these; we went to different runaway shelters; we put out posters, and were constantly looking up and down streets to see if we could see her. Day after day, we tried to find her but to no avail.

It didn't take long for me to get to the place where I enjoyed not having her around. I was extremely relieved, but my husband and children were dying inside. I worried about Rose, but trusted that the Lord was caring for her wherever she was. But I was not able to show my elation because of my family's sadness.

I know many of you believe that if you could just get rid of your husband then all your discomforts would go away. Much like Rose running away, you have a great need for some relief. But I must tell you that Rose was a

Bichon Frise puppy and a puppy is much different than a husband. Puppies will come and go, but God desires that you not go through husbands like pets. He desires for you to have one husband until he, or you, dies.

There is usually a reason for sicknesses that attack our good health. When you feel a cold coming on, you realize that you may have overworked you body and need extra rest. So you pack in the vitamin C and go to bed early to get a good night's rest. What a cold causes us to do is rectify the reason that brought on the illness in the first place. It causes us to slow down and care for ourselves.

When our children get colds, we spend extra time taking care of their needs. We awake from a restful sleep to check their temperatures. We want to guarantee that the fever doesn't go above a certain point. We stock up on medicines, juices, and chicken broth. We make available all the supplies necessary to get them well.

When our daughter, Ravin was just five weeks old, I noticed she began to nurse differently. She never got a full meal but would fall asleep nursing in a very short time. After a few days, I noticed she began to have a lot of mucus when she spit up. She was baby number seven and I assumed that she had caught the bug going around the house.

One morning, I got up to force her to eat. I needed milking and she was the reason these buckets were overflowing. This particular morning, she ate better than she had all week, and I was so pleased. But after about ten minutes, she threw up everything mixed with tons of mucus. Then my little nine-pound, five-week-old baby went limp.

I ran to awaken Ray. We loaded everyone in the car and rushed to the nearest hospital. Ravin was then transported, by ambulance, to Children's Mercy Hospital. On the way, the technicians had to stop to stabilize her twice. When we arrived, it took about two hours before the doctor came to the waiting room to give us the news. She had RSV (Respiratory Syncytial Virus—a virus that produces microorganisms in the upper and lower respiratory tracts in infants) and had to be placed on a ventilator.

The doctors told us that they would do all they possibly could to help. Putting her on the ventilator allowed the machine to breathe for her, so all of her energies could go to healing her body.

On that very morning, I had food supplies in my home to prepare for a funeral repast at our church for one hundred people. When Ravin got sick, I called other members of our church to prepare the meal while I attended to our little one.

When we have problems in our marriage that result in us becoming Sick of our Spouse, we must put all things aside. Just like when church members came to my aid when Ravin was sick, others are capable of picking up some of the things on our agendas so we can tend to this sickness that is contaminating our intimacy.

The Path Toward Sexual "Healing"

When we get to the point where we wish that our spouse would run away and never return, we need to put everything else on hold and put all of our energy into healing our relationship. When we feel a cold coming on, we take extra care of our bodies and rest more often in order to heal. Yet, we allow our marriages to somehow muddle through, never taking the time to care for the sickness that is slowly taking its toll on our relationship.

Most of us understand why we are in the state we are in. We have valid reasons, and most have to do with our husbands. We are certain he will never change, and because of this, we are destined to remain in a state of being sick of spouse. If only you could change all the things that you don't like about him! Because you cannot, you feel stuck.

Just for a second, I want you to think about all the things you do in a day that you don't feel like doing. Most of us get out of bed every morning even though we feel like staying in. We get dressed and go to work, even though we would rather have the day off. How many times a day do we answer the telephone and talk to someone we don't feel like talking to?

As we get in the car after work, our eyes are on the prize: home. We don't feel like stopping at the traffic lights, or getting out of the way of that emergency vehicle. When we are home, we don't feel like fixing dinner, but we do.

Now, let's take the time to think about what would happen if we didn't do the things we didn't feel like doing. Staying in bed constantly because you didn't feel like getting up is called depression and there is help for those who suffer from depression.

If we decided to just skip work for no reason, we would expect that we might get fired.

Think about the chaos if we were on our way home and some other car decided they didn't feel like stopping at their red light. After we slammed on the brakes to avoid the ensuing accident, we would roll down our window and scream to the top of our lungs, "Are you crazy?!" (Okay, maybe you would thank God for protecting you...I would, but after the window was rolled down and those words were on the other side of my lips!)

To be sick of spouse and not do anything about it is a mental illness. No one would continue to live in pain if they have the ability and knowledge to alleviate it unless they were mentally ill. To intentionally harm oneself is mental illness. Allowing your marriage to remain in a state where you have issues with your spouse and do nothing about it is living with avoidable pain. We must get to a place where we will take time out of our busy schedules to nurse our marriages back to good health and alleviate pains that could be eliminated.

The only one capable to fight for healing in the sick of spouse area is you. If you're incapable, you have to have others around who are willing to pull you to safety and get you the help you need that you don't have the ability to get for yourself.

To allow yourself to remain sick of spouse, you must mentally checkout of the relationship or become comfortable with spiritual mediocrity. God says in 1 John 4:20, "If anyone says, 'I love God,' and hates his brother, he is a liar; for he who does not love his brother whom he has seen cannot love god whom he has not seen. And this commandment we have from him: whoever loves God must also love his brother." Therefore, if you remain in a state of being sick of spouse, you are sick of God as well.

God does not leave you without a way to return to relationship with Him or your husband. Luke 6:27 says, "But I say to you who hear, Love your enemies, do good to those who hate you, bless those who curse you, pray for those who abuse you." Start out by loving your husband the way God loves. 1 Corinthians 13 says love is patient and kind. You must do good to him. God shows us this also in Jeremiah 29:11 by example when he says that He is about "doing good and not harm" and in Proverbs 31:12: "she (the wife) does him good, and not harm, all the days of her life." Then we must bless our husbands by speaking well of him. It is difficult to have an issue with someone whom you talk about positively. Begin to tell your husband all the things that he does right.

The enemy will allow you to see and focus on the things that your husband does wrong. He wants you to only notice his shortcomings because that allows you to remain sick of your spouse. If you remain in this mindset then your relationship doesn't bring glory to God, and that is exactly what the enemy wants.

There are specific things you can do that will put you on the road to healing your intimacy issues. The first is to pray for him. It is impossible to pray for someone that you are sick of without your genuine prayers either changing them or you. Another is that you have to feed him and give him drink (Proverbs 25:21 and Romans 12:20). No strychnine or poison.

God's ways are not our ways (Isaiah 55:8), so the exact opposite of what we feel like doing is often what God asks us to do. And one of the things God knows better than we know is that we cannot continue to be sick of spouse if our focus is on serving God. Begin to serve God with passion and you will begin to serve your husband without animosity. One of the biggest factors in our not continuing in the cycle of being sick of spouse is that we are not seeing our husband as more significant than ourselves.

Do nothing from rivalry or conceit, but in humility count others more significant than yourselves. — (Philippians 2:3)

JOURVOTIONAL

Sick of Spouse

1. If you were completely honest and were guaranteed no one would ever see what you wrote, what are some things that make you sick of your spouse?

_____

_____

_____

_____

2. Some of us married with no sickness but have developed hang-ups over the years. Throughout your marriage, what do you think has caused these sicknesses, if any, to occur?

_____

_____

_____

_____

3. List the responsibilities (for you and your husband) that cause you to muddle through in marriage and not take the time to nurse your marital ailments.

_____

_____

_____

_____

_____

_____

4. Specifically list 5 things you do in a day you would rather not do.

_____

_____

_____

_____

_____

5. Are there areas where you feel like God has disappointed you or you feel disappointed by God? Explain.

_____

_____

_____

_____

6. Read the following scriptures and give your thoughts on their meanings:

1 Corinthians 13:4

_____

_____

Proverbs 31:12

_____

_____

Luke 6:27

_____

_____

How can you apply these verses to your marriage?

_____

_____

_____

_____

_____

_____

_____

7. Read Philippians 2:3 and fill in the blanks.

> Do _____ from rivalry or
> _____, but in _____
> count others more _____ than
> _____.

How can you apply this scripture to your life and marriage?

_____

_____

_____

_____

_____

S.O.S. — CHAPTER #12

SICKNESSES OF SEX

Husbands, love your wives, as Christ loved the church and gave himself up for her, that he might sanctify her, having cleansed he by the washing of water with the word, so that he might present the church to himself in splendor, without spot or wrinkle or any such thing, that she might be holy and without blemish. — (Ephesians 5:25)

185

Many women who are sick of sex and not wanting to change their view of sexual intimacy have been subjected to so much pain in marriage. There are many things that plague our marriages and in order to be an over comer and begin to wage war against these ailments, we must first be able to identify what kind of sickness continually troubles us.

For healing, we treat a common cold much differently than we would treat pneumonia. Some of the troubles that have attacked our marriages need different treatments than we have used before to bring about healing. Just as there are diverse reasons why we are sick of sex, there must be different ways we go about healing our sicknesses.

There are basically four different categories that our "Intimacy Sicknesses" fall under and there are many twists on our painful experiences that fall under these categories. Primarily our issues with sexual intimacy are because of physical, mental, emotional, or spiritual pain.

Physical Sickness

Every intimacy ailment has a cure in Christ Jesus. There are some that are just plain tougher to overcome than others. To have physical pain tied into your intimacy, is one, I believe, of the hardest.

(In some cases physical pain has medical causes in sexual intimacy. There are some lubrication issues that cause severe pain. If KY jelly doesn't help, please consult your ob/gyn or a Christian sex therapist).

Physical abuse, rape, unpleasurable intercourse, or even abusive intercourse can get you to spiral down a path that causes you to harden your wounded heart to ever believing that sexual intimacy can be enjoyable and holy. Each of the reasons you or anyone you know falls into this category may leave you never wanting to even try to find safety in sex. For some wounded in this area, it is repetitive and repeated by the one who is supposed to be your protector.

Any husband who causes his wife pain, either physically or sexually is not a husband that is biblically obeying God and His Word. The Bible says, "husbands, live with your wives in an understanding way, showing honor to the woman as the weaker vessel, since they are heirs with you of the grace of life, so that your prayers may not be hindered" (1 Peter 3).

Every intimacy ailment has a cure in Christ Jesus.

Your husband may not even have the desire to live with you in an understanding way. His most major issue begins with his own personal relationship with Jesus Christ. And that is where you must begin to get the necessary cure for this sickness that is dominating your marriage.

Your Pathway to Healing #1: Forgiveness

The hardest thing to do in this human life of ours is to forgive someone who continually hurts us. In Matthew 18:21, Peter is trying to understand all the teachings of Christ and what it will take to have the heart and mind of Christ. He knows that traditional rabbinical teaching says to forgive an offense of another three times and on the fourth there will be no forgiveness. Peter knows, because he has walked with God, that he must go the longer mile and so he says, "Lord, how many times must I forgive my brother who sins against me? As many as seven times?"

Jesus tells Peter that we must exercise our forgiveness to an even greater measuring rod. He says in verse 22, "Not seven times, I tell you, but seventy times seven!"

Now, you may be counting because your desire is to be a woman of the Word and your husband may be at offense number 489 and you know he will make 490 by the end of the week. But, God is not asking us to count offenses here, he is asking us to infinitely forgive and the only way you can do this is by seeing your husband the way Christ does. This forgiveness doesn't mean you forget these acts of violence that continually hurt you. It doesn't mean you should stay and allow yourself to be physically or sexually abused, but it does mean that you must continue with an attitude to forgive his every offense against you.

Forgiveness is what will completely heal you from the physical sickness that was heaped on you. You will become a daily reflection of Christ to your husband. This is truly a picture of grace to your husband for you to become a tangible picture of Christ to him, reminding him of God's love and forgiveness.

A man that experiences this repeated forgiveness will be a man that esteems and honors the one who has granted him this forgiveness. True, it may take years for him to truly see your selfless gift of forgiveness to him. But God asks us to forgive as long as it takes-seventy times seven.

In Luke 7, a Pharisee named Simon asked Jesus to have dinner with him one evening. Jesus went to his home to have dinner and a woman (who is said to be of the town but also described as a sinner) heard that Jesus was dining there came with an alabaster jar of perfumed oil. As she stood behind Jesus, she began weeping and her tears wet his feet. So moved by Jesus, and not having a cloth with her, she wiped his feet with her hair, kissed them, and anointed them with the sweet smelling oil. Now when the Pharisee that invited Jesus to come saw this, he said to himself, "if this man was a prophet, he would know who and what kind of woman this is who is touching him that she is a sinner." Jesus then posed a parable of sorts to Simon:

> A certain creditor has two debtors; one owed
> him five hundred silver coins and the other

fifty. When they could not pay, he canceled the debts of both. Now which of them will love him more? Simon answered, "I suppose the one who had the bigger debt canceled. Jesus said to him, "you have judged rightly." Then, turning toward the woman, he said to Simon, "Do you see this woman? I entered your house. You gave me no water for my feet, but she has wet my feet with her tears and wiped them with her hair. You gave me no kiss of greeting, but from the time I entered she has not stopped kissing my feet. You did not anoint my head with oil, but she has anointed my feet with perfumed oil. Therefore I tell you, her sins, which were many, are forgiven, thus she loved much; but the one who is forgiven little loves little." — (Luke 7:41-47)

By continually forgiving the afflicters of our hurt and pain, we are able to experience the continual forgiveness of God to us. His forgiveness is sure. His forgiveness is without conditions. His forgiveness is infinite.

Mental Sickness

The most common of the sicknesses against our intimacy is mental sickness. Mental illness is any of a number of various disorders characterized primarily by abnormal behavior or an inability to function socially.

I believe mental illness is the most common sickness because our intimacy is threatened mostly by what we think and believe. Our personalities are reflected by what we think and believe also.

In our marriages, we have neglected to build each other up. When we begin to build anything, it usually takes more time and effort than we knew it would take when we set out to do our project. That is the same thing that happens when we are called to build each other up. It takes more time and effort than we knew it would take when we said, "I do."

In Ephesians 4, Paul lays out some of the gifts God has given to the saints to build up the body of Christ. In the same manner, God has given you as a gift to your husband to build him up. It may not be reciprocated, because often times when someone does not feel good about themselves, they have a tendency to put those around them down or not say anything at all to build any one up.

If your husband has a poor view of himself, he cannot see himself in the light of Christ's view of him. A man with a poor self-image probably won't have a whole lot of positive things to say to you. Many things in our childhood are "caught" and not "taught." He may have never seen anyone build up another and he may never have caught the vision for this. You have been put together to teach him to build up and not to tear down.

But, you are his gift—given to build him up so he can do the task God has for him to do. You may be one of many women who are living with a husband who continually tries to crush every fiber of your being. You have lived with this mental abuse so long that you never expect him to change. He continues to mentally tear you down or does nothing at all to build you up.

God tells us how to live with this man. He gives us a remedy to overcome the mental sickness that your husband intentionally or unintentionally continues to heap on you. Begin by memorizing Luke 6:28(ESV) 'bless those who curse you, pray for those who abuse you.'

Your Pathway to Healing #2: Prayer

Jesus tells us in Matthew 5:43-44, "You have heard that it was said, 'you shall love your neighbor and hate your enemy.' But I say to you, Love your enemies and pray for those who persecute you, so that you may be sons of your Father who is in Heaven." God asks you to pray for him. I know there are those of you who have prayed and want to give up but prayer is sometimes a long process.

There was this crazy old woman in our church when I was growing up. Almost every Sunday evening, the deacons would lead in a devotional and they would have popcorn testimonies. Popcorn testimonies would get everyone up, quickly, to say something good about the Lord. Everyone would try to hurry and give their quick testimony before this lady because there was no one who was brave enough to follow her.

That crazy lady's name was Nannie Babe Hughes and she was my daddy's mother. Yes, my grandmother was the laughing stock of all the young people in my church. When her turn for testimony arrived, she would stand and begin by quoting Psalm 103, "bless the Lord, O, my soul: And all that is within me, bless His holy name. Bless the Lord, O, my soul and forget not all his benefits." By the time she squeaked out the word, benefits, she was shouting, from the tops of her lungs, all the kindnesses that God had shown her and she was thanking Him with exuberance! She would walk up and down the aisles of the church stopping to touch somebody and tell them that God was "sweeter than the honey in the honey-comb."

When I was older and had become a Christian myself, I began to spend more time with my grandmother. One day, I asked her why she shouted like a crazy lady when it was testimony time. She explained to me just one of the reasons that her joy was so full. There was an occasion where her husband wouldn't allow her to go to church. He felt like she was needed at home so he told her not to go. She wanted to honor her husband so she didn't go to church. But, not wanting to miss time with God, she began having church at home. She would kneel to pray in her living room, Sunday after Sunday. God allowed her to see all the benefits that He has kindly given to her and she began to thank God, she thanked Him with the same energy and fervor that she did at church. It wasn't long before her husband begged her, "Go back to church, Mrs. Nannie. Go back to church!"

My grandmother understood that *prayer changes things!* And she was going to pray until her change came. With enthusiasm!

Emotional Sickness

Emotional sickness comes when busyness keeps us from showing emotion, one way or the other, about desiring intimacy with our husbands. When you get to a point where you really don't care about the state of your marriage, you have embraced an apathetic view of intimacy.

God tells the Laodicean church that he will spew them from his mouth because they are neither hot nor cold (Revelation 3:15). They were lukewarm spiritually and were content with their wealth, yet unaware of their spiritual need.

Emotional sickness is portrayed when we are content with our busyness and not concerned with our marital need. Emotional sickness can be present in a marriage for years before we get to a point where we tire of the lack of concern for the state of our marriage. Sadly, this form of sickness is one of the biggest teachers of our children. We teach them through our unconcern for our marriage that it is okay to exist together and be emotionally absent from another. This indifferent response to our marriage plunges us into the final sickness that keeps us Sick of Sex.

Your Pathway to Healing #3: Believe

There are so many areas that are attacking our marriage intimacy, that we are, oftentimes, incapable of believing things will ever change. In times like these, I remember one of my favorite verses, Philippians 4:13: "I can do all things through Christ who gives me the strength."

One of our biggest downfalls that the enemy of our martial intimacy continues to plague us with is in the area of our faith. He does everything he can to make us believe lies when all we need to remember is that God is able to do exceedingly, abundantly ABOVE all that we can ask our imagine (Ephesians 3:20).

Too many marriages are falling apart all around us because one of the spouses has great *belief*—belief that God *can* do anything *except* this one thing. To get the sickness out of our marriage and get us on to the pathway of healing, we must believe that God can do ANYTHING!

Healing means we must go through the process, learning each day that we have a trustworthy God who desires to give to His children good things. You must believe, as a child of God, that God wants to give a marriage of great intimacy to you.

Spiritual Sickness

When you ignore the many sicknesses that ail your marriage, it catapults you into the most devastating sickness of all. Spiritual sickness will ravage a marriage of all the benefits due you. Spiritual sickness causes those in a marriage to not have a standard. When you are at a point where you don't care about your physical, mental, or emotional wellbeing, your spiritual wellbeing is soon to follow. When spiritual sickness becomes your way of life, you begin to deteriorate because your accountability to God wanes.

When you are content with being spiritually sick, this not only plagues your marriage but sends you down a totally different road of having your entire life plagued. You will not only be sick of sex, you will be indifferent towards life. God is the one who keeps us upright. If you are not in a growing relationship with Him, you will slowly deteriorate into not caring about anything at all.

We have to identify these threats to our marriages. We have to find the appropriate cure for these threats and we must constantly work to make sure these threats are rendered incapable of getting us back to a place of apathy again.

Your Pathway to Healing #4: Faith

The final pathway to intimacy is faith. Faith is an action. As you take all four pathways, (first to forgive, secondly to pray, third to believe), your fourth pathway gives you the ability to take action because you have faith in someone greater than yourself.

Faith is what it takes to take on marriage in the first place. Marriage is risky. It means two people have to adapt to one another in such a way that onlookers see them as one. So in order for you to get to that place after you have taken the first three pathways, you must know that your faith is in someone who will NOT fail you. Your faith must be in God, the author and finisher of faith.

Since God, in His mercy, has given to you a husband, He is gracious enough to walk with you, daily, through all your marital situations. But you must have faith to trust Him with every aspect of your marriage. The faith that you have in God gives you the strength to get up every-day and fight for your marriage. You must know that God is already victorious over all that attacks you, so you are already a winner. Your marriage intimacy is a testimony of God to a world that is looking for a Savior.

This faith in God gives you the power to get back in the ring of marital intimacy every time you are thrown out. The enemy of God will make sure you will have some bumps and bruises but God is creator and inventor of the salve that CAN HEAL every bump and bruise. He is F-forever, A-available, I-internally, T-to, H-help. He is FAITH.

> For we walk by faith and not be sight. — (2 Corinthians 5:7)

JOURVOTIONAL

Sicknesses of Sex

1. Identify the ailments that constantly trouble your marriage.

_____

_____

_____

_____

2. Which of the four categories of pain, physical, mental, emotional, or spiritual, do your specific ailments fit under and why?

_____

_____

_____

3. In looking at your constant ailments above, your forgiveness pathway to healing must begin by you forgiving what?

_____

_____

_____

4. Your second pathway to healing is prayer. Write out your prayer to your Heavenly Father about each particular marital ailment. Remember, He is our GREAT PHYSICIAN.

_____

_____

_____

5. When there is a continual pain, we sometimes believe that this pain will be constant forever. Do you believe that God can alleviate your pain and completely wipe it out? _____

6. Now briefly describe what your life would look like if these particular ailments were no longer a part of your marriage.

_____

_____

_____

_____

_____

7. Read Hebrews 11:1-3. Answer the following questions.

· Faith is the assurance (evidence, being sure, substance, being certain). What does assurance mean in your marriage?

_____

_____

_____

· The Bible also described faith as the EVIDENCE of things not seen. What does evidence mean in your marriage?

_____

_____

_____

· Matthew Henry states that "Faith demonstrates to the eye of the mind the reality of those things that cannot be discerned by the eye of the body." Write out specifically what faith means to you.

_____

_____

_____

8. Spend time in prayer regarding your faith. Allow time for the Lord to encourage you knowing that He is capable. Meditate on Jeremiah 32:17: "Ah, Lord God! Behold, You have made the Heavens and the earth by Your great power and outstretched arm. There is nothing too hard for You."

Simple Ways to Begin Healing the Sicknesses of Sex

1. Make your marriage a priority of your daily prayer time. PRAY CONTINUALLY AND FAITHFULLY FOR YOUR MARRIAGE.

2. Begin to pray, every day, for your spouse. That he would hunger and thirst for God.

3. Memorize Matthew 5:6.

S.O.S. — CHAPTER #13

SINS OF SEX: PART I

Therefore God gave them up in the lusts of their hearts to impurity to the dishonoring of their bodies among themselves, because they exchanged the truth about God for a lie and worshiped and served the creature rather than the Creator. — (Romans 1:24-25)

Have you ever wondered how a Christian can remain in blatant sin? I have thought to myself, "How can these Christians say they love and obey Jesus though their attitudes and actions say exactly the opposite?"

I had a very good friend many years ago. We were both Christians and so excited about conquering the world for Jesus. She met this really nice guy—and soon after began a sexual relationship. Within a couple of months, she was pregnant. With this unplanned baby, she decided to have an abortion. I begged her not to and even asked her if I could go with her to Planned Parenthood. I thought if I was there, she would not be able to go through with this and kill her baby. But she absolutely refused for me to go with her. She knew what she was doing was wrong. She told me "God will forgive me" and went ahead with the abortion and then went on vacation to "get away from it all."

A lot of times I look at people who *know* they are doing wrong and question, in my mind, whether they *really* have a personal relationship with God. I used to find myself judging people on what they did or didn't do to determine their walk with God. You know, I elected myself a judge to God's court system. I have since come to conclude that we often find ourselves overlooking sin because we see no other option. We know God is a forgiving God and we count on His forgiveness time and time again. We must understand that, yes, God is a forgiving

203

God and once we have repented, He sees our sin no more, but the repercussions of our sin are left to us to daily walk out and walk in the consequences of these sins.

My dear friend had an abortion because she saw no other option. If there had been a way to keep the baby and not have to deal with the minister father, the church body, and all the other complications, I am sure she would have kept her baby.

When we see no other option, we take matters into our own hands. But how we handle our affairs must line up with God's truth. In order for us to come to terms with what a "right" sexual relationship looks like, we must discover if we are living with a false imitation of a true sexual relationship. We must expose the lie with truth.

Prior to marriage, the sin of sex is exploited in many ways. This includes pornography, fornication (pre-marital sex), masturbation, lust, and many more.

Pornography: A Sin of Sex

Pornography often seems to be harmless, but it directly goes against scripture. In Matthew 5:28 it says, "whoever looks on a woman with lustful intent has already committed adultery in their heart." God is always concerned with your heart. Pornography has a way of grabbing on to your heart and not letting go. The only intent of pornography is to cause sexual arousal with someone you are not married to.

In Song of Solomon 2:7, 3:5 and 8:4, we read, "I adjure you, O daughters of Jerusalem, by the gazelles or the does of the field, that you not stir up or awaken love until it pleases." God warns us three times about the heartache that comes from pre-married sexual arousal. This sexual heightening through pornography will dull your standard for sexual purity. So to get you in his clutches early, the enemy uses magazines, pictures, movies, lyrics, books, newspapers, commercials, and more to numb your mind to God's caution for immature sexual arousal.

We may not think just a look is wrong but soon, a look is no longer all you will desire. Pornography is addicting and it will plummet you into premarital sex or sexual addiction in marriage.

Pornography is sin. To participate in pornography in any way is dishonoring God and your husband. There are many men (and women) who are addicted to pornography and it is causing sickness sexually (and sexual death in our marriages). To continue to view the images that cause you artificial sexual stimulation is to disobey God. It causes your intimacy to have sickness. James 5:13-16 says, "Is anyone among you suffering? Let him pray. Is anyone cheerful? Let him sing praise. Is anyone among you sick? Let him call for the elders of the church, and let them pray over him, anointing him with oil in the name of the Lord. And the prayer of faith will save the one who is sick, and the Lord will raise him up. And if he has committed sins, he will be forgiven. Therefore, confess your sins to one another and pray for one another, that you may be healed. The prayer of a righteous person has great power as it is working."

Do not let your pride keep you from seeing this sin of sex and calling for help in your marriage. Confess your sin of pornography with someone you spiritually trust so healing can take place. Pornography needs to be driven out of our marriages and this begins with prayer and confession.

Pre-marital Sex: A Sin of Sex

Pre-marital sex is a sin of sex often accepted by the world and Christians alike. But, premarital sex is blatantly opposite of what scripture tells us is right for a follower of Christ. To be sexually involved, prior to marriage, is to disregard biblical boundaries. These boundaries are established by God to keep you pure. We have fallen for a lie and many of us believe there is no way we can live without sex even though we are not married. But we can. In 1 Thessalonians 4:3-8, the Bible says:

> For this is the will of God, your sanctification: that you abstain from sexual immorali-

ty, that each one of you know how to control his own body in holiness and honor, not in the passion of lust like the Gentiles who do not know God: that no one transgress and wrong his brother in this matter, because the Lord is an avenger in all these things, as we told you beforehand and solemnly warned you. For God has not called us for impurity, but in holiness. Therefore whoever disregards this, disregards not man but God, who gives his Holy Spirit to you.

For the past fifteen years, Ray and I have been speakers for the FamilyLife "Weekend to Remember Conferences." Our speaker's retreat is held often in St. Petersburg, Florida. It is held at a beautiful resort and is surrounded by white sandy beaches. Every day we have a chance to swim, sit on the beach, enjoy drinks from the cabana, hang glide, you name it; we are able to participate in the activity.

A few years after attending these retreats and loving every minute of it, we had the privilege of facilitating a conference in Jamaica. We were in an all-inclusive resort on the oceanfront, and the beaches were indescribable. Every luxury you could imagine was at our fingertips. We took long walks on the beach next to the clear ocean waves; we drank strawberry daiquiris and piña coladas while resting on beach lounges. Even to this day, Jamaica remains a sweet memory and I think about it often. I long to visit Jamaica again.

This is what premarital sex does to you. It makes you long for Jamaica, when everything was just fine in Florida. Jamaica is like a benefit of marriage. To be actively sexually involved outside of marriage causes you to forsake the beauty of Florida and indebt you to what is in Jamaica. "Florida is alright, but you haven't experienced anything until you visit Jamaica!"

As a Christian, when you participate in sex before marriage, you and your husband will have to deal with the effects of this sin in marriage. Every sin, though cleaned by the blood of Jesus, has consequences. One of my friends always wonders if her husband married her because they were having sex or if he really loved her.

Jamaica is fine for those who are privileged to experience it and can afford to go with someone they have committed their life to in marriage. Jamaica is a blessing to them. Just as sex in marriage is approved and honoring to God. But for those who would have to go into debt to experience Jamaica, Jamaica would become a curse. After visiting and incurring the debt, you will long for it; it will call you and will often feel like you cannot live without visiting Jamaica again.

But your visiting of Jamaica was under false pretense because it caused your debt. Sex, prior to marriage, is false intimacy and opens a door to extreme debt against your own body. When you are sexually involved prior to marriage, the desire for intimacy makes you want more and more. This is similar to incurring more debt. You want something that you are not in a position to obtain. And the consequences for getting it anyway far outweigh the benefits of owning or having it.

Visiting Jamaica when you could only afford Florida, or having sex without marriage makes a wonderful place and memory lose its beauty. The sin in continuing to be sexually involved is that you become a slave to the debt of premarital sex. (And debt, in any form, always requires a payoff).

For those of you who have been or are involved in pre-marital sex, remember God is a redeeming God. He desires you to be Holy as He is Holy. When you came to Him and accepted His free gift of salvation, He saved and cleaned you from all sin. Now it is time for you to represent Him with your body. Ephesians 5:8-11 says, "For you were once darkness, but now you are light in the Lord. Live as children of light (for the fruit of the light consists in all goodness, righteousness and truth) and find out what pleases the Lord. Have nothing to do with the fruitless deeds of darkness, but rather expose them." Or as my Momma used to say, "When you see the light, walk in it."

Pre-marital sex is a fruitless deed of darkness. The enemy of Christian marriage wants you to believe that to be involved sexually prior to marriage has no ill effects. This is deception and will rob both you and your future husband. Christ has paid your debt and wants you to enjoy intimacy with Him, and only with who He brings to you as your life-long mate.

So even though you may have sinned in this area, it is never too late to make a commitment to save yourself for marriage going forward. The benefits for you, your future spouse, and your marriage are well worth the wait and you are worth waiting for.

Masturbation: A Sin of Sex

Masturbation is a sin of sex that many don't feel is wrong. Many Christians have been counseled by well-intended Christian leadership to masturbate to keep you from pre-marital sex. Masturbation only involves you, and you may think there is no harm done but oh, there is. It hurts you because it allows you to simulate the sexual act that God intended to be for two.

Masturbation by definition is erotic stimulation of one's own genitals, commonly resulting in orgasm achieved manually or with instrumental manipulation.

God never intended sexual intimacy to be for your own pleasure. He created sexual intimacy to always be for two, male and female. That is why he created two people with two distinctly different sexual parts to come together for pleasure. Masturbation, like pornography, steals a part of your heart and perpetrates shame.

Masturbation is not an option to obtaining sexual control over your body prior to and during marriage.

Lust: A Sin of Sex

Lust, like masturbation, is only for the pleasure of one. When God created sexual intimacy, he created it for the pleasure of two that have become one. Lust is more than a look. Lust is using your mind to think of intimate acts with someone who is not your spouse. To look at someone and recognize that God's creation is beautiful is different than lust. Lust is an intense desire or a sexual appetite for a woman or man who is not your spouse.

Sins of Sex in Marriage

Just as there are counterfeit sexual sins prior to marriage, there are false pretenses in our marriage beds as well. These are the things that constantly plague your marriage but you pretend they are irrelevant to your intimacy with your husband. These often leave you believing that they are not a contributing factor to why you are sick of sex with the one you have committed to until death do you part. They are adultery, emotional affairs (even with your girlfriends or mother), and the absence of sex in

211

marriage. These are just a few of the sins of sex that the enemy of intimacy uses to keep our marriages in mediocrity.

Many believe that marriage is the solution to loneliness. But you can be married and be even lonelier than when you were single. Marriage is not the cure to any ailment that plagues your intimacy. But these contributing factors are some of the pretenses that keep our marriages mundane.

Adultery: A Sin of Sex

Adultery is sex between two people when one or the other is married to someone else. An adulterous relationship is deceitful, fraudulent, and always divisive. The heart of one spouse is divided because of a physical relationship with someone else. Adultery is so despicable to God that it is one of the Ten Commandments (Exodus 20:14). Over and over in the Bible, God warns of the entanglement of adultery; yet it continues to entrap more people. How are we protecting ourselves from adultery? Proverbs 6:32, "He who commits adultery lacks sense; he who does it destroys himself."

When you physically commit adultery with someone, you choose to believe the lie of the enemy over believing the truth of God. A fool is a person who will believe and act on a lie when they know the truth. To commit adultery is to play a fool to Satan. It divides your marriage and makes no sense. It is entrapment at best and death to your intimacy with the only one you were meant to have exclusive intimacy with.

Emotional Affairs: A Sin of Sex

Just as with adultery, an emotional affair divides the heart of one of the spouses in a marriage. God intended for married folks to have unity and not division. In an emotional affair, you long to spend time talking (emoting) with someone other than your spouse, and it occupies your mind. You cannot wait to converse with this person and your conversation, with them, is fulfilling to you. This contradicts scripture and causes division. God wants us to "leave and cleave" (Genesis 2:24).

Emotional affairs are more common among women than with men. Women are made for relationship. Just as our husband's sex drive should drive him to intimacy with us, our need for relationship should drive us to intimacy with him. Often because of the work involved in relating to our husbands, we choose an emotional affair with someone else. We can continue an emotional affair for years and call it "chattin' with my best friend." But an emotional affair or what we'd also call an abnormal emotional attachment is a relationship that involves sharing intimate details with someone other than a spouse.

When something great happens, whom do you want to share it with? Most of us would say, "My husband," but a lot of us would say, "My husband, _____, and _____."

If you have to talk intimately, debrief, or unwind with someone every day, even if it's your mother, more than likely you are involved in an emotional affair or have an unhealthy emotional attachment.

Often times in marriage, we even make our relationship with our children unhealthy by substituting emotional conversation with them instead of our husband. Emotional affairs are unhealthy for any relationship that is determining to experience godly intimacy with your spouse. You have an emotional bond with this other person, and it does cause division between you and your spouse. If it has not already caused division, it soon will. And if it does not appear to cause division, then there is already a division problem. You are involved in an emotional affair if you must talk with someone every day or talking to that someone is on your mind every day. (Other than the Lord).

Each of these affairs causes division in our marriages and division in our relationship with God.

> *Let your fountain be blessed, and rejoice in the wife of your youth, a lovely deer, a graceful doe. Let her breasts fill you at all times*

with delight; be intoxicated always in her love. Why should you be intoxicated, my son, with a forbidden woman and embrace the bosom of an adulteress? For a man's ways are before the eyes of the Lord, and he ponders all his paths. The iniquities of the wicked ensnare him, and he is held fast in the cords of his sin. He dies for lack of discipline, and because of his great folly he is led astray.
— (Proverbs 5:18-23)

JOURVOTIONAL

Sick of Sex: Part I

1. Can you think of a friend who says they are walking with God but are making or has made some non-biblical choices? What were these choices and why are they not biblical?

_____

_____

_____

_____

2. What are some non-biblical choices you have made since becoming a believer in Jesus Christ?

_____

_____

_____

3. Do you have any Sins of Sex that were a part of your life prior to marriage? What were they?

_____

_____

_____

4. If you have not already, take time to go to God right now and ask Him to forgive you of these sins.

5. What are some of the consequences of you participating in these things prior to marriage?

_____

_____

_____

_____

6. In your marriage, can you see some things that could cause mediocrity in your intimacy?

_____

7. When you have great news to share, list the people you would like to immediately share your news with.

_____

_____

_____

Examine each of these relationships. Is there a potential for an emotional affair or codependency in any of them?

_____

8. Thinking about your marriage, what are some areas or things that could cause division between you and your spouse?

_____

_____

_____

9. Read Proverbs 5:18-19. What is God saying to you and your spouse in these scriptures?

_____

_____

_____

_____

What does the last sentence of this scripture mean: "may you ever be intoxicated by her love," "be exhilarated always with her love," "may you ever be captivated by her love"?

_____

_____

_____

_____

10. Pray to your Heavenly Father that your marriage would be one that would be mutually fulfilling and that your husband would always be captivated, exhilarated, and intoxicated by your love and that this would be mutual.

S.O.S. — CHAPTER #14

SINS OF SEX: PART II

"For by the grace given to me I say to everyone among you not to think of himself more highly than he ought to think, but to think with sober judgment," — (Romans 12:3)

For Christians, some of us are just too puffed up. When I couldn't understand how my friend could have an abortion, I wondered about her personal relationship with Christ. We have secretly become judges of ourselves and others. We think that our heart is right with God because we are not actively participating in pornography, adultery, emotional affairs, lust, or masturbation. We absolutely know that we are not sinning because sin is all that stuff.

But there is a large group of Christian women who are being deceived. I am one of them. We believe that since we occasionally give in and give him what "he" needs that their sexual intimacy is okay. Since we are not out having sex with the mailman, after all; and you won't find the Internet Porn, Pornographic magazines, or "X" rated movies in our homes. We wanted a pure relationship with God and our future husbands, so we waited until marriage to have sex. We once held sex in high esteem.

That was then, this is now…

There is a sin of sex that, in my opinion, is just as big as all the others mentioned in the previous chapter. This sin is so big because so many of us don't even realize that it is sin. It is often bigger because it is so accepted in our society though, I believe, it grieves God immensely.

1 Corinthians 7:5 says, "Do not deprive one another, except perhaps by agreement for a limited time, that you may devote yourselves to prayer; but then come together

again, so that Satan may not tempt you because of your lack of self-control." This sin is to not have sexual intimacy in marriage. (I am speaking to Christian marriages with no medical complications, mental, or physical challenges). To refuse to have regular sexual intimacy with your husband in marriage is sin. It is sin against God and His Word.

> *To refuse to have regular sexual intimacy with your husband in marriage is sin. It is sin against God and His Word.*

God has such a high standard for sex in marriage that the only biblical reason not to have sex is a fast. He said, "Do not deprive one another." God compares the deprivation of sex in the same way He uses the deprivation of food. These fasts are used to set aside a time to commit to prayer. This means sex should be as regular in your diet as the sustenance of food. We can go a few days without food, but without necessary nutrients and hydration, our bodies tire and become weak. There are people depriving themselves of food and it is a mental illness called anorexia. When a woman or man allows this condition to continue, they will have organ failure, and their bodies will wither away.

This is the same with sexual intimacy with our husbands. Both our bodies are meant to have this necessary connection. Without it, the relationship grows weak, and we easily tire of and get frustrated with each other. It also causes relationship failure and intimacy withers away.

God tells us that to withhold from sex should be "by agreement for a limited time," so to not have sex should be agreed upon. Then it should be for a limited time. Limited marks a boundary of time before complete restoration. Sex does not have to be every day, but sex with your husband should be regular.

What is regular to you? Ask your husband what is regular to him. Once or twice a year is not regular, that's annual or semi-annual. It's called a holiday. (I know some of you just closed the book because now you have to think of something else to give him for his birthday or Christmas!)

There are many reasons why we have lost our desire for sex with our husbands. One common reason is we are downright fatigued with all that we deem necessary to get done each day. We think, "He is a grown man, and sexual intimacy with him will have to wait." But Satan has tricked us with all the fatigue: we are not accomplishing much, even though we are so tired. We are in more debt, our homes are in shambles, and we have no authentic relationships with those in our homes or at work. We are tired, but we have nothing eternal to show for our fatigue.

After talking with one of my friends, I realized that another reason we tire of sex has to do with the guilt carried after many years of being sexually active prior to marriage. She and her husband were both Christians and knew having sex was wrong. But she felt that if she stopped having sex then, it would hinder or even break the relationship. As she shared with me how this made her feel, she said, "What is the difference? He was the leader in the relationship before we got married, and he knew sex was wrong. Yet, he continued to have sex with me. And now he is the leader in the relationship and sex is right." She cannot overcome the switch that was to take place and how her husband made the change so quickly. She still lives with the sin of that premature, inappropriate relationship every time he touches her. She cannot get over the fact that he was the leader and was willing to compromise when it was convenient prior to marriage, and now he is unwilling to compromise after marriage, "He wasn't supposed to then and did—but now I am supposed to, and I don't want to."

Overcoming an inappropriate introduction to sex plays an important role in our difficulty to appreciate sexual intimacy today. We are finding out that rape, abuse, incest, and feeling pressured to have sex to keep a boyfriend or just to be close are more prevalent in our families than we really care to admit.

In order to have a good sexual relationship, we must get the sin out of our sex. Greg Speck, a world-renowned speaker to youth, says, "Good sex is not primarily the results of positions, technique, or experience. Good sex is primarily the result of a loving, committed marital relationship, and that takes no experience."

The biggest reason that we are having intimacy issues with our husbands is that we give and take sex away depending on how we feel. We feel like if we have to have sex, then he'll get to on "my terms."

I was at a restaurant with three of my best girlfriends when we began a conversation about sexual intimacy with our husbands. During the course of our dialogue, one of my friends said, "Robyn probably never turns Ray down." This conversation was the first time I realized there is more than one way to reject your husband sexually.

Ray has never experienced sexual rejection from me when he is in my good graces. Even when I am tired, I tell him to give me a couple of hours of sleep and I will "keep my promise." But there have been numerous occasions when I have rejected him. I just didn't say it with words. There have been many nights where I allowed the sun to go down on my wrath and positioned my body so Ray absolutely knew that nothing—not even forgiveness—was taking place that night. If his tiny, baby toe just accidentally touched mine, I was sure to move all the way over to the edge of the bed. In my anger, I forfeited a good night's rest and my portion of that king-sized bed for a tiny corner, just to make sure no part of his body touched mine.

This sin of sex is the ultimate killer of marital intimacy because it is justified to us. Satan has us believing that it is our right to deny sexual intimacy because we are mad about something. He has us believing that it is okay to deny sex and allow the issue to go unresolved for a good night's sleep, but no one is sleeping. You are both too angry to sleep.

When I was about ten years old, I had a friend who played at my house quite a bit. My mom didn't appreciate this friendship because she saw that this friend was manipulative. If she didn't like the way things would go (and they always had to go her way), she went home. I always wanted her to stay because she had a lot of great toys and took them all with her when she would leave. She was the typical "I-am-going-to-take-my-ball-and-go-home-if-you-don't-do-what-I-say" girl.

This is the illustration that God has given me each time I am on the edge of my bed. I am taking my toys and leaving because I didn't like something Ray said. But every time my friend abruptly left, I wanted to still play with her. I felt rejected. I found myself doing the same thing to my own husband that my friend did when she rejected me.

This is what we are doing to our marital intimacy. Their sex drive pushes them to sexual intimacy with us. In some cases, he desires sex with you so he knows your relationship is okay. How would you feel if he decided he was tired of being rejected, on and off again, and just wanted to find someone willing to always share her toys?

Many of us would fly to the church and confess: "He's sharing his 'toys' with someone else," failing to mention all the countless times he wanted to play with you and you refused to play.

Sex is not some tool of vengeance. It is not something you can give and take back at will. If your husband normally has a right to play with your toys anytime, he should be able to play with your toys all the time.

Remember that 1 Corinthians 7:5 says, "except perhaps by agreement for a limited time, that you devote yourselves to prayer." God, then, makes it clear why adding this sin of sex to the mix will harm your intimacy. The end of that same verse reads, "but then come together again, so that Satan may not tempt you because of your lack of self-control." Sooner or later, one of you will lack self-control. Satan will make sure of it.

God has given us the gift of sexual intimacy to freely give to or husbands and allow both, you and him, to give and receive pleasure with each other. But we are allowing the enemy of our godly marriages to enter our bedrooms and make us hold out on sexual intimacy because of anger or control.

When Satan enters your bedroom and has you and your husband divided, that situation needs to come to a quick resolution. You may not see eye to eye, but you still need to know that nothing should divide your relationship. The ultimate test is when a situation has not come to your desired conclusion, can your husband still approach you sexually and be received?

Intimacy of some sort should culminate every battle, so you declare to the enemy (and to each other) that your relationship is stronger as a result of this hurdle. I am finding that when Ray and I fight, a simple kiss goodnight (and to this date he has not rejected my kiss nor I his), lets me know we will overcome this hurdle. Make the enemy run from your bedroom and do not allow him to relax and be comfortable on a well-built perch.

Experiencing sexual intimacy the way God created it to be guarantees sin will not enter your bedroom. If you have areas of premarital sexual sin, get help to abandon them. Begin by asking God to forgive you, your husband, or anyone involved. Then grasp forgiveness and remember you are forgiven. Once you have sought forgiveness, you need to have an S.O.S.—Sold Out Sister—someone who will pray for you and hold you accountable.

Sexual intimacy was never meant to be a gift to give and take at will.

If you have areas of marital sin that continue to creep up, some helpful tools for you would be a married group study in your church. Even a neighboring church may offer something your church may not offer. We need support in breaking down some of the built-up barriers in our marriages. (Look for a couples Bible Study in your area, or begin one with friends.)

227

God wants every marriage that wants to bring honor to Him to have unhindered, loving sexual intimacy. God cannot remain in the middle of sin. We have to clean out our sin closets. Some of our closets have a lot of untouched stuff hidden in the backs of them. But we must unpack all our all baggage.

I realized one day that my friend who always took her toys and went home had to feel the same way I did. She had no one at her house to play with, and she always came back to play with me. Having toys and no one to play with is lonely. Just as lonely as giving and taking sex because of how you feel. Sexual intimacy was never meant to be a gift to give and take at will. This is ultimately an issue of control. When the battle for control enters the marriage bed, we begin to treat each other like we are enemies.

> Holding out on sex is selfish.
> It is sin.
> It is self-centered.
> And it is wrong.

We will answer to a Holy God who is the giver of all good and perfect gifts, and sex is one of them.

> *"He reveals deep and hidden things; He knows what is in the darkness, and the light dwells with Him."* — (Daniel 2:22)

JOURVOTIONAL

Sick of Sex: Part II

1. Do you believe to not have regular sex in your marriage is disobedience to God and His Word? _____

2. Think about your intimate relationship with your husband. What are some things you know you have done right in your intimacy? (Examples could be: no affairs, never turned down his advances, or have a nice atmosphere for intimacy.)

_____

_____

_____

_____

_____

What are some things you see that needs to change?

_____

_____

_____

_____

3. What are some ways you work out your conflict, tiredness, or anger so that sexual intimacy is a regular part of your marriage?

_____

_____

_____

4. What are some things you believe a sexless marriage lacks?

_____

_____

_____

5. The times when you have not had regular sex in your marriage, was it agreed upon by you and your husband for a limited period of time? What was the situation? How long was the deprivation?

_____

_____

_____

6. What, if any, are some of the things in your schedule that keep you fatigued and too tired for intimacy?

_____

_____

7. Greg Speck says, "good sex is the result of a loving, committed marital relationship." What is your personal definition of good sex?

_____

_____

8. What are some conflicts, frustrations, or things that cause you to not want intimacy with your husband?

_____

_____

9. Has there been a time (or two or three) where you have had a conflict and wanted to take your "toys" away?

_____

10. What did you immediately do to either justify your feelings or combat that desire to withdraw intimately?

_____

_____

11. At the end of a conflict with your husband, what is your way of making sure you both know that your relationship will be stronger as a result of this hurdle?

_____

_____

_____

12. To hold out on sex is a battle for control. Read 1 Corinthians 7:5 again. Write, in your own words, what you know this scripture is saying to you.

_____

_____

_____

13. Spend some time in prayer asking God to give you the strength to avoid denying sexual intimacy with your husband. Seek Him to remove the pride and allow you "not to think of yourself more highly than you ought to think, but to think with sober judgment."

Ways to Begin to Overcome Sins of Sex Affecting Your Intimacy

1. Confess this sin to someone. Shame is broken when someone knows your secret.

2. Memorize Psalm 23:3.

3. Remove from your home, work, etc., anything that would cause you to continue in your sin area.

S.O.S. — CHAPTER #15

SURRENDERING OUR SOULS

*He restores my soul. He leads me in the paths
of righteousness for his name's sake.*
— (Psalm 23:3)

You may have wondered, "Can I ever express my discontentment?" In the "Shamed of Shape" chapter, we talked about contentment. Embracing contentment in your marriage relationship is displayed in freedom. Grasping contentment with your body shape allows you to be satisfied with who you are. Living in a relationship you are completely content in gives you peace of mind. But there is a time for discontentment.

The enemy of marriage wants us to focus on all the circumstances, conditions, and things that would lead us to discontentment. He wants us to have areas in our lives that we feel are unfulfilled. But there are certain areas that if focused on, the discontentment will drive you to want more.

There is a time for discontentment. There are two areas where discontentment is imperative. This should be in our two deepest, most intimate relationships. We should never live content in our bond with our husband or with God. If you become content in either of these two relationships, complacency will creep in and will spiral you again into discontentment. Wanting more out of proper, intimate relationships will cause you to desire deeper intimacy. You will go to all lengths to get it, and that is what makes you passionate.

Christian women will go to women's retreats, women's bible studies, seminars, small groups, and many other venues to enhance relationships. But when we attend these events, we must go with a heart of anticipation, wanting to learn or gain something we've never heard before. Once we hear what God has for us to hear, we need to be impassioned to allow Him to accomplish it through us. We know that when our relationship with God is vital and growing then everything else will fall into place. Even if whatever He is asking of us seems impossible, we know "His grace is sufficient for you, for my power is made perfect in weakness" (2 Corinthians 12:9) because, "I can do all things through Christ who strengthens me (Philippians 4:13).

Desiring more out of your relationship with Jesus will drive you to a more passionate relationship with Him. To desire more out of your relationship with your husband will drive you to a more passionate relationship with him. Passion in any relationship cannot be hidden. If you are passionate about God, a searching world will know it. When you are passionate about your marriage, you will not have to mention it; it will be evident for all to see— especially your husband!

In order to get to a place where you want more, you need to be willing to risk what you already have. *Passion about something makes you so fired-up to achieve what you desire that you are willing to surrender what you have in order to get what you want.*

Most women are comfortable with the relationship they have with their husbands. We are complacent about continuing to pursue an even deeper connection with him. We are comfortable about the information he shares with us and are not willing to risk asking more to draw him out. We desire a deeper level of intimacy but are not willing to fight for it.

Ray was talking with Dennis Rainey, co-founder of FamilyLife Ministries, and sharing with him a passion that God placed on his heart. Dennis said, "Ray, dreams are cheap, but implementation is costly."

Are you dreaming of a deeper level of intimacy with your husband? It is time to stop dreaming and do whatever is necessary to get it. *Implementation is costly!* You want him to relate to you more? Talk to him more so that he becomes comfortable talking to you. I know this is hard to do but we need to get to the place where we ask more than one question before we can truly hear his heart. It is easier sometimes to sacrifice the time and energy to understand and know our children, but are we willing to sacrifice to understand our husbands?

There is only one way to get to a place where we are comfortable with sacrifice. First, we must surrender to an ongoing intimacy with God. Far too often, we become comfortable with our relationship with God. We hear what we want to hear and this type of hearing drives us to complacency.

We must never get comfortable with our relationship with God. We must desire to know more about Him and

His ways. Begin this by memorizing scripture and learning to talk to God more by praying all the time (without ceasing). By placing action to your desire, passion will be ignited.

Become Discontent with Complacency

Satan, the enemy of godly marriages would have every Christian marriage content with complacency. Complacency means "self-satisfied and unaware of possible dangers." Our enemy wants us to be self-satisfied and unaware of possible dangers in our marriages. We have become so comfortable with the state of our marriage that we have no idea that our intimate relationship is stagnant. If we remain complacent, our marriage becomes mediocre. Mediocrity breeds only adequate marriages, not great ones.

Likewise, our homes are filled with a lot of things that display our financial success but we want them to display our spiritual depth as well. To have this takes a daily surrender of our will and a desire to have God's will.

Surrendering is one of the most difficult things we will ever do. To surrender means to give up. The only time you give up is when you have realized you cannot win on your own. To keep your intimacy in marriage alive, you must surrender your marriage to God, often. This means that you must be willing to relinquish your possession or

237

control of your marriage. You must be willing to abandon and relinquish the power of your marriage to God, as a prisoner would. Prisoners usually have no choice but to obey those in command. You have to become a voluntary prisoner—giving up not only your life, but your soul.

Our soul is the part of our life that is eternal. It is the part that stands before a Holy God and gives an account for the life that we lived. Our soul is the makeup of who we are. It is the part that makes you a person with a personality and not just a shell of a human. It is the part that will hear: "Well done, thou good and faithful servant."

Because of the loose culture in today's world, our children are not seeing the need to marry or pursue intimacy. Yet we know that they cannot truly live without it. Satan wants us to remain mediocre in marriage so that he can pounce on our children and trounce our legacy. He wants to make marriage ineffective and he is doing it by allowing us to become content with an average relationship. He wants Christian marriages to become extinct. He is trying to do this by wiping out Christian marriages through the mediocrity of intimacy. This will slowly remove the visual reflection of Jesus' love for His church on our children and society because marriage is a picture of this love.

Killing Complacency

In order to win this battle of complacency, we must first be willing to surrender to God, who has already won this battle for us. He is victorious and has given us the victory. First Corinthians 15:57 says, "But thanks be to God, who gives us the victory through our Lord Jesus Christ." Victory is played out in front of us, everyday, in different venues and games.

I love the summer Olympics. I am enamored by the track and field events. In a hypothetical game, let's imagine runners are ready at the starting line. The gun goes off and one of the runners takes off and is way in front of the others. He crosses the finish line in first place and begins to cry and wail. The sportscaster comes, with excitement, to him and begins to interview him in the instance of his emotion but soon finds out that the runner is very angry. He is in the middle of pitching a fit.

> "Why are you so angry?" the dumbfounded sportscaster asks.
>
> "I lost this race!" wails the first-place finisher.
>
> Trying to salvage his interview, the sportscaster points, "Everyone is cheering for you! You crossed in first place. You won

239

this event! Let me be the first to congrat-
ulate you!"

"I don't want the medal. I didn't win,"
says the runner and he runs out of the
arena.

Would you understand this behavior? No, you would
not. But this is our response to what Satan is doing to us.

Are you living with a grateful heart knowing you are
victorious or are you living with the belief you have
failed? Defeat for Christians is confusion because you are
already victorious! Remember that 1 Corinthians 14:33
says, "for God is not a God of confusion,
but of peace." As victors, what do we have
to surrender? Not only our lives but our
souls.

By surrendering your soul to God, you receive one thing: God's perspective on your feelings.

What is the difference between our
lives and our souls? Both coexist here on
Earth, but the life has a beginning and end,
the soul is eternal. Your soul is the moral
and emotional nature of who you are. It is
the place where emotion and sentiment get their origins,
and it is the place that will make you fight for what is
important to you.

Because emotion and sentiment get their origins from
your soul, by surrendering your soul to God, you receive

one thing: God's perspective on your feelings. Most of us live by how we feel. Unfortunately, we are only feeling what we selfishly emote. We must allow God to wrap our emotions in the covering of His blood. It will change your point of view as soon as you get a feeling and desire to want to respond incorrectly. By surrendering your soul, you become a godly responder.

To be a godly responder takes one thing. TIME. Throughout our day, we must take the time to connect with God about everything. This is how we "Pray without Ceasing" (1 Thess. 5:17) by running each area of our lives through the divine wisdom of God and responding to please Him. It takes supernatural ability to do this, and this ability only comes when you are in constant communication with the One able to give you the power to respond correctly. God is our power source.

You must live in full surrender to Christ who has the power to overcome Satan. Romans 12:21 says, "Do not be overcome by evil, but overcome evil with good." Well, Satan is evil and God is good. By surrendering your soul, you will have the power to not respond and remain angry with an improper perspective. Surrender your soul and you will be able to overcome the evil that the enemy tries to make you feel you have the right to feel. Satan will become powerless to you.

When you surrendered your life to Christ, you became a new creature. It changed all that you were.

241

Christ gives you the power to de-clutter your mind, attitude, and your schedule. You are new! But the surrender of your soul requires daily denying of yourself as we see in the Matthew Henry Commentary on Mark 8:34, "Whosoever will come after me for spiritual cures, as these people do for bodily cures, let him deny himself, and live a life of self-denial, mortification, and contempt of the world; let him not pretend to be his own physician, but renounce all confidence in himself and his own righteousness and strength, and let him take up his cross, conforming himself to the pattern of a crucified Jesus, and accommodating himself to the will of God in all the afflictions he lies under; and thus let him continue to 'follow me;' as many of those did, whom Christ healed. Those that will be Christ's patients must depend on him, converse with him, receive instruction and reproof from him, as those did that followed him, and must resolve they will never forsake him."

The only way to surrender your soul is to daily die to self. This was such an important message that God, the Father, gives us the same message in Luke 9:23, Luke 14:27, Matthew 16:24, and Matthew 10:35.

Selfishness and surrender cannot co-exist. When you wake up and find yourself beginning to think about how you feel, you are walking in selfishness. Soul surrender is not taking place. When your husband does that little thing (and you know exactly what it is) and it gets on your last nerve…what is your first response? Soul surrender has taken place when you can stop and ask Jesus how to handle this emotion and not respond the way your flesh wants you to.

How I am learning to surrender my soul every minute of every day? I am not Ray's enemy. I am given to him so that when he falls, and he will, I am there to lift him up and vice-versa. By the surrendering of our souls, we become strengthened with power through the Holy Spirit, and we will be able to understand and know the love of Christ that is above knowledge (Ephesians 3:16). Surrendering our souls transforms us from being selfish to becoming selfless. It takes the "what about me?" out of our situations and changes our view to "what about God?" The surrendering of your soul is probably one of the hardest things you will have to continually do because it requires laying down your pride.

When Ray and I first married, I wanted to go to a midnight madness sale at a department store. I was going to meet two of my sisters there and we were going to "shop 'til we dropped."

Telling Ray my plans for the evening, he responded with "I don't think that is wise." This began a major argument about whether I was to go or not. At the end of the conversation, Ray, exasperated, said something like, "I am your protector and if you won't listen to me, I leave you in the hands of the Lord." WHAT? I was furious! I felt, at the time, that I didn't have to listen to Ray but I knew I must listen to God. I knew God would not be in the midst of our confusion and it meant I needed to submit to the God-given authority placed in my home. I didn't like it one bit but I knew that having my own way was the beginning of an unhealthy pattern being established. As I slept on the corner of my bed that night, I knew I must surrender my soul. I had to stop and ask God to help me handle this destructive emotion that had me angry enough to "greatly dislike" Ray that evening.

I chose soul surrender that night and God covered my pride with His love. Ray is my gift from God. He is my protector and friend (even when I don't like what he thinks he is protecting me from). I could either continue to fight my best friend that evening or I could surrender and see what is more important: my way or God's way?

I used to be a woman who thought she would never let a man tell her what to do. I am now a wife who seeks the counsel of my husband about most every major decision I make. There is safety in counsel and Ray's counsel has saved me from being overwhelmed on numerous occasions.

Soul surrender makes you a woman who is more concerned about God's image than your own. It is saying in your heart just as Jesus said in Luke 22:42: "Father, if you are willing, remove this cup from me. Nevertheless, not my will, but yours, be done." By surrendering your soul, you are able to see God's hand in every area of your life. God wants to do great things in and through our marriages. Are you willing to surrender your soul so He can?

Now to Him who is able to do far more abundantly than all that we ask or think, according to the power at work within us.
— (Ephesians 3:20)

JOURVOTIONAL

Surrendering Our Souls

1. What is the last event, get-away, or retreat that you attended?

_____

What was your take-away from this event?

_____

_____

_____

2. What is the last event you attended just to focus on your marriage? (Family vacation doesn't count.)

_____

What was your take-away from that event?

_____

_____

_____

3. When is the last time or date you had with your husband?

_____

4. When is the last planned prayer time or "date" you had with God?

_____

5. List some relationship areas you would like to see grow with your husband.

_____

_____

_____

_____

6. List some relationships areas you would like to see grow with God.

_____

_____

_____

7. What are some things you are willing to sacrifice that you already have to get to the intimacy you desire with God and your husband? (Examples might be less time with your children, less time in front of the TV, cutting back on your work hours, etc.)

_____

_____

_____

8. What miracle(s) would need to take place for you to be able to relinquish the areas in #7?

_____

_____

_____

_____

9. What are some things you have given up (surrendered) to achieve a deeper relationship with God and with your husband?

_____

_____

_____

_____

_____

10. List one success (victory) you have had in your marriage. List one success you have had with or for God.

_____

_____

_____

_____

_____

11. Read Mark 8:34. Write specifically what that would look like for you.

_____

_____

_____

_____

_____

12. What are your pride issues that you must lay down so you can surrender your soul?

_____

_____

_____

_____

_____

13. Read, again, Ephesians 3:20. Meditate on it and then pray that God will do in us "more abundantly than all that we ask or think, according to the power at work within us."

Simple Ways to Begin Surrendering Your Soul

1. Identify one area where you are just accepting a situation/relationship and write out what it would look like if it was exceptional.

2. When you are getting ready to respond to something, really ask yourself, 'What would Jesus do?

3. Memorize Psalm 139:14.

S.O.S. — CHAPTER #16

STRONGHOLDS OR SAFETY

For the weapons of our warfare are not carnal, but mighty through God to the pulling down of strong holds…
— (2 Corinthians 10:4)

I was casually talking with one of my dearest friends on the phone about this book and the need for it. I began telling her about this chapter, and how I saw Satan's continual tactics in the area of sex. I shared about Ray's sexual abuse as a child and my own misperceptions about sexual intimacy that have caused us to fight for it in our marriage. Then my friend, very matter-of-factly said, "I was raped in high school, and I felt like I was ruined for life. It caused me to think that I had to sleep with a man to keep him around" (see Olivia's story).

I sat with my mouth wide opened on the other end of the phone. This was not some casual acquaintance; this was my true-blue friend! We have been through so many things together, and she is the one who would actually tell me if I hurt her feelings and expected an apology. But this was the first time she had ever shared this part of her life with me, and we have been out of high school over thirty years!

This one conversation led me to begin asking those close to me to share their introduction to sex and how that one experience formed their sexual views. What I found was that some of us have had sexual experiences so unpleasant that we have no hope of sex ever being a beautiful thing. Things so tragic that we would rather never speak of it again—in hopes that the pain would go away, and there would be no distinguishable lasting effects. These experiences shape our views because in trying to escape the pain, we have avoided true intimacy. Not just with our husbands, but in every relationship.

Sexual sin or misinformation about a loving sexual relationship touches every life. Rape, abuse, incest, wrong information, pornography, sexual promiscuity (and countless other things), are travesties that are real and leave big, open wounds. These wounds are the direct result of our choices or the choices of others. No one volunteers to be raped; no child willingly walks into molestation, yet bad things continue to happen to good people. Sin is real, and no one is exempt from the stains of it.

When I first became a Christian, I heard Christians who had been saved longer than I had say that when someone continued in a certain sin, that the sin was a "stronghold." At that time, I understood that this was a sin area that was so tough for this Christian to break away from. It would always be a battle. These strongholds leave stains and the stains keep us guarded. There is no way to erase the stain; it can only be covered. Stains, if uncovered, keep the victims hindered and responding to life with guarded hearts. These uncovered stains create a negative stronghold for us.

Living with a guarded heart keeps you trying to protect yourself from hurt ever happening to you again in this certain area. As the old Chinese proverb goes, "If a man fools me once, shame on him. If he fools me twice, shame on me." Guarded hearts and self-protection keeps the stain of that sin ever before you. It keeps you so focused on the promise to yourself that this will never happen again that you misdirect your attention. Your attention must be kept in trusting the almighty God and not in yourself!

But our strongholds do not have to be negative. There is a place where a stronghold is safety. According to the Merriam-Webster dictionary, a stronghold is a fortified place, a place of security and survival. In the Psalms, God is referred to as the Stronghold—the place of security and survival for the believer. God desires to be your stronghold—your place of security and survival. He will take that ugly stain that you don't know what to do with and not erase it, but cover it with His love.

Satan has tricked us into responding to our lives with fear because of this sin that has touched us. He wants us to remain bound by this "stronghold" causing us to fear and live gripped by this sin. But God, being our stronghold, allows us to see no fear. First John 4:18 says, "there is no fear in love, but perfect love casts out fear. For fear has to do with punishment, and whoever fears has not been perfected in love."

Satan has us believing that God cannot be trusted. After all, He allowed this bad thing to happen. Yes God allowed the sin, but He did not perpetrate the sin. His allowing the sin does not negate His goodness. God can be glorified in our response to sin. Run to Him and He will be your stronghold. *But God can only be the stronghold if you allow Him to be.*

Here, again, we see the enemy of our life and soul, stealing something that we rightfully own. God is our Stronghold. The day you placed your life in the hands of God, He became your stronghold. Believing anything other than what God says to be true becomes a noose around our neck—slowly getting tighter to cut short your hope. Believing that your issue with sex will never change or that you will never be free to love the way God intended, is believing a lie. Remaining in that lie takes the stronghold of sex from where it is safe in God to being unsafe within you. Satan not only wants you to see sex as an area you will always have to contend with, he wants you to believe that God is not the place of safety in this area.

If you have come to a place where you believe you know best how to handle any area for you to be able to live with it, then the sin, itself, becomes your stronghold. What you must do is determine that God is your only hope, allow Him to be your stronghold—your place of security and survival and He will be your place of safety in this area.

In the area of sexual intimacy, these youthful strongholds are continuing to render us vulnerable. Mostly because these strongholds are established when you are young and don't have the spiritual wisdom, knowledge, or courage to fight against the lie.

God wants you to return to Him as your stronghold. Yes, God had the power to stop the sin that was waged against you—He also had the power to stop the sin waged against Him, on the cross—but He allowed it and wants you to respond to it by bringing glory to Him.

When Daniel was placed into the lions' den and the three Hebrew boys were placed in the fiery furnace, I am sure they didn't understand why these things were perpetrated against them. They were serving the living God. But God used this to prove His greatness.

God is your stronghold and He leaves you with a tangible reminder of how safe and secure His arms are. This token of God's safety is found in the arms of your husband.

God Grants Safety Through Pure Sexual Intimacy

When you arrive at a place where you decide you are not going to live with the lie of that sin that has touched you, you choose safety. God, in his divine wisdom, has placed a safety belt right in your home. It is there to protect you from dangers, both seen and unseen.

When you get ready to go for a drive in your car, you put on your seatbelt in case there is an accident. After a while, it becomes automatic to put on your seatbelt. You make sure anyone riding in your car buckles up. This seatbelt does not prevent an accident, but it is an extra measure of protection when there is one. Every time you drive, there is a possibility of being involved in an accident.

Our husbands are placed right there in our homes to be a seatbelt for us. Because of sin, Satan has us believing that we need to protect ourselves and there is no safety with our own husbands. Satan attacks our homes with intentions to harm us. But within the arms of your husband, there is safety. Just as the seatbelt, his arms wrapped around you will guard and protect you from the dangerous lie of believing that intimacy with him isn't sacred.

Begin enjoying sexual intimacy in the arms of your husband and watch the lie disintegrate. Sometimes, this takes time as this deeply embedded lie is being replaced with truth. But we need to fight for the truth and never surrender to the lie.

There was a time in my marriage when because of Ray's past sexual abuse, sex became a time of emotional pain for him. He kept assuring me that it wasn't me, but it sure seemed like it was. Sexual abuse, for the victim, places them in a huge "fear" hole. You cannot expect a victim of a crime to accept anything that reminds them of the crime enacted against them, without pain. Healing from this pain takes time, effort, surrender, and a loving, confidential friend to help the victim climb out of the hole the enemy has kept them in.

When we were in seminary, Ray went for counseling. I wanted to help him so much but didn't know where to start. During that time, the Lord gave me a way to help Ray by fasting and praying for him. I used to fast and pray, just for Ray, each Monday morning until lunchtime. As I prepared breakfast for the kids, I would forfeit mine and ask the Lord for mercy on behalf of Ray. I wanted his pain to be relieved and I wanted him to be all that God would have him to be. In our years of safety in our own marriage and our commitment to each other, the scars of that abuse are no longer present in our sexual intimacy.

Years ago, Ray determined to seek freedom in the arms of God. He granted forgiveness to those who perpetrated the sin against him (though they never asked to be forgiven) and found safety and security in the loving arms of Jesus. Ray chose to believe God. And instead of believing the lie that Satan was trying to build in him, Ray humbled himself before God and walks with Him in His security and survival, everyday. It has granted him peace, a rich marriage, and true intimacy.

In a similar way, I had to determine that I would not make Ray live with the effects of my guarded heart. My heart was so guarded as I viewed the many failed marriages around me. It caused me to only trust me and "protect" myself. I had to learn to find safety in the arms of my imperfect husband, Ray. And in turn, Ray has also found safety in my arms, his imperfect wife.

When you find safety in your home, you will find security there. When a place is a place of security, every inhabitant of that place is set free.

> *The name of the Lord is a strong tower; The*
> *righteous runs into it and is safe.*
> — (Proverbs 18:10)

JOURVOTIONAL

Strongholds or Safety

1. What was your first introduction to sex?

_____

_____

_____

_____

2. Was this introduction a positive or negative experience?

_____

If negative or untrue, how have you emptied this untruth so you can respond to intimacy in truth?

_____

_____

3. List one time where you have seen God as your stronghold.

_____

_____

_____

4. Read Proverbs 18:10 again. Write this verse from your Bible and comment on what it means to you.

_____

_____

_____

_____

_____

5. What are some safe and secure things in your home?

_____

_____

_____

_____

6. What are some of the things that the enemy has tried to establish in your home to make you believe that God is not your stronghold (your place of safety and security)?

_____

_____

_____

_____

7. Spend time praying about each of these things before God. When you run to Him, you are safe.

Simple Ways to Begin Establishing Safety in Your Intimacy

1. Ask your husband to write down one thing you can begin praying about for him.

2. Share one small thing with your husband that you may not have thought to share with him before or have been ashamed to share with him. If he will, pray together after this time of sharing.

3. Memorize Isaiah 26:3. Creatively post this scripture all around your home.

S.O.S. — CHAPTER #17

STEALING OUR SEXUALITY

The thief comes only to steal and kill and destroy. I came that they may have life and have it abundantly. — (John 10:10)

261

Sexuality is the quality or state of being sexual. Many of us don't realize that long before we understood sex, our sexuality was being stolen. Satan used several devices to diminish your sexuality.

My mother is a dynamic woman who raised ten children. Her own mother died when she was eight years old, and she had absolutely no intimate relationship with her step-mother. Still, my mom made each of us feel special. She made clothes for us for Easter and decorated cakes for each birthday. She was very involved in our high school and made every visitor to our home feel like she had personally invited them.

She was also a talker. She could hold a conversation with anyone, and they felt like she was interested in every word they had to say. But there was one area where mom didn't have much to say: S-E-X. When we were growing up, it was difficult for mom to talk about such things. But when we were older, there were a few things mom had to say about the matter and they weren't very positive.

My mom made sex seem like it was a dreaded requirement of marriage. She referred to her own sexual intimacy as being "your Daddy's sleeping pill," "A hand in the dark," or a "Wife's duty." These were just some of the things that mom used as her secret code for sexual intimacy. But these things stuck with me.

I am sure that sex was not all bad for my mom, but who was she supposed to talk to openly about sex? It was a very hush-hush subject in her day. Sex was not talked about by my mom's peers, and it was certainly not a topic of conversation with her sisters or step-mother. Only the "bad" girls talked openly about sex, and they weren't talking to the "good" girls. So Mom had to learn about sex through her experience with Daddy. Whether sex was bad or good, Mom never had anyone she could talk to about it. Resources on sexual intimacy were not as readily available and the women in the church would never talk about "such matters."

Some of my friends' moms said things like: "Sex is a no-no" as if they were talking to toddlers, and my grandmother would say things like: "Keep your legs crossed at all times when you go out." Some of these things are said in jest or embarrassment. Most of the things our parents said were meant to dissuade us from becoming sexually involved before marriage. The things that Mom said were harmful but the things that Mom *didn't* say about sex may have been more detrimental than the things she did say. As parents, we have come up short in that area of walking our children though a godly preparation for sexual intimacy.

My mom never talked to me about sex. I left home for college at seventeen and lived on my own or with other people until age twenty-six. About two months before my wedding day, I moved into my parents' old home with my Mom to begin the final preparations for my wedding. Mom came into my room one night and sat on the side of my bed. I knew she wanted to talk but what was she to say? By that time, my view of sex and my own sexuality was already established.

We have to be proactive in our approach to sex. Our children need to get a godly prospective about a God-created love. Too many of us are leaving our children's sexual education up to the school, peers, or luck. It is our responsibility, as parents, to give our own kids the right perspective of God's purpose and plan for sexual intimacy.

Remember what Greg Speck said, "Good sex is primarily the result of a loving, committed marital relationship and that takes no experience."

How the Christian Parent Must Stop This Thievery

As Christian parents, we must take the initiative to launch our children into a healthy sexual relationship in their marriages. What our parents said or didn't say created either a distorted view of sexual intimacy or a solid launching pad for us. The launching pad we give our kids will either offer them a proper, healthy view of sexuality, or an improper one. The more we talk openly about sexual intimacy in our homes, the more opportunity we create to see what views our children have. These conversations give us the opportunity to give direction to our children and weed out false information.

Watching movies with our children is another way to initiate conversations of sexual intimacy. We were recently watching a movie and my twenty-one-year-old daughter Raychel had her roommate over from college. My daughter Rhesa was five at the time and in the room coloring a picture. There was a scene where the husband and wife were obviously going to become intimate and even though they cut to the next morning, Raychel thought it was the perfect time to make a joke. She said, "Rhesa, go to school and tell your teacher that your mommy and daddy have s-e-x." Of course, the room exploded with laughter thinking that Raychel had just got a good joke over on Mommy and Daddy. Ray sat there laughing with the kids, and I came back with, "Rhesa, tell your teacher that mommy and daddy have s-e-x, o-f-t-e-n!" I laughed so hard at my own joke that we missed the next fifteen minutes of the movie.

> *The more we talk openly about sexual intimacy in our homes, the more opportunity we create to see what views our children have.*

We all have established views on sex and many of us need to start over to eliminate our own false information. We must seek a right perspective on this "intimacy thing" because it is at the core of our marital relationship.

Momma should have told me that sex was created by God to bring honor to Him and for our pleasure. She should

265

have told me that sex was only the icing on the marital relationship and my marriage relationship was the cake. And barring any mental or physical ailments, icing is nothing without the cake.

Momma should have told me that sex would be a lifetime of growing together with one man. It would include passion, laughter, excitement, and routine. But all are needed to see intimacy endure.

Momma should have told me that there would be times when sex wouldn't be as important to me or to him. Things come up like fatigue, lack of communication, work, illness, or other issues. She should have told me that these times come in every relationship and that is normal.

Momma should have told me that there are different seasons of sexual pleasure. She should have told me to anticipate these seasons and be grateful for them all.

Momma should have told me that in order to have a proper view of sex, I had to have a proper relationship with her, Daddy, and God.

Momma should have told me that God is the creator of all things new. He is capable of restoring and rebuilding sexual intimacy between two people who are seeking Him.

Momma should have told me that when things are right with God, and He has restored everything, sex is better and more abundant than I could have asked or imagined it to be.

Momma should have told me that it is never too late to see "old" become "new." And that God can and will restore sexuality.

Momma Who?

Many of us, now as Christian women, look at the Proverbs 31 woman and wish for the day when we meet her standard. She makes exotic food for her family and sews all their clothes by hand. She gives to the poor and needy and her household is ready for every season. She is an entrepreneur with several diversified businesses.

Today, this is nearly unthinkable. Clothes are readily available to purchase and all kinds of foods are at our neighborhood markets. There are shelters and welfare for the needy, and we dust off or buy new winter coats every year.

As a mom of nine children, I understand the pull of all that has to be done to maintain a family. And, on top of it all, money is never available in excess. College, growing kids, and groceries take the excess. Many moms, including me, have been forced to work to be able to provide the things that are needed.

Because of all the demands, those long, intimate talks with your children are a distant memory. Modeling sexuality to our children is a good thought, but there is no time to really invest in a good picture of it.

Single motherhood and the absence of mom, when helping provide for the family, is a way our sexuality has been stolen right out from under us. When mom and dad are away providing, we need to question who is modeling sexuality to our children.

We are sexual beings. In order to have a proper view of sex, you have to understand and appreciate the female and male species. Girls need women and mothers around them to properly see the model of their future role. Boys need men and fathers around them to, see masculinity modeled before them, of their future positions.

Yes, we financially provide for our kids but have we left them deficient in the area of godly role models? We must always question "Who is watching our children?" or "Who are we allowing our children to watch?"

When we left our homes of origin, how prepared were we to delve into marital and sexual intimacy? How are we intentionally and purposefully preparing our own children to have a healthy awareness of their sexuality?

In the midst of us financially providing for our children, we MUST be godly role models for them. To be available to our children, even when we must provide financially for them, we must ask ourselves these questions: "How much time does my job/outside activities rob me from my being a tangible role model?" and "What can I realistically eliminate now, so I can be the primary influence in my own children's lives?"

Daddy Who?

All women have a need for a nurturing, proactive, godly father-image in their lives.

Marriage represents the image of God and His love for the Bride, His church. So Satan has waged war on the family and has marred it in a way that could render it helpless. This warfare has removed fathers from the home through divorce, death, single-parenting, and abandonment.

In order for us to recapture sexuality, we must accept that sexuality can only be recaptured by each of us having a proper perspective of men. For our children to recapture sexuality, they must have both male and female

269

interaction and relationships. Without both, we are packing our children unhealthy baggage for them to unpack in their own marriages later in life.

We must learn to love men. We must learn to believe the necessity that men and women are different and love that God created us this way. I know we believe that we love our husbands, but do we love men? In 1 Corinthians 13:4-8, "Love is patient and kind; it is not jealous or conceited or proud; love is not ill-mannered or selfish or irritable; love does not keep a record of wrongs, love is not happy with evil, but is happy with the truth. Love never gives up; and its faith, hope and patience never fail. Love is eternal." This kind of love grants men the freedom to be men. Not to be like women in any way.

Men and women are different in their responses, thoughts, and nurturing. Satan uses these differences to isolate us from one another and offer us the tendency to disrespect men and men to disrespect women. (He uses this as the main reason for divorce. We file our decrees under the heading of "Irreconcilable Differences.") We will always have these irreconcilable differences as long as we are male and female. The only thing that makes them reconcilable is the glue of Jesus Christ.

Satan has stolen our sexuality by building a disrespect of the male species deep within us. To not understand why our husbands do what they do makes us not trust them. There is no way we can respect someone we don't trust or trust someone we can't respect. If you have any issue with men or masculinity, sexuality cannot be restored without first changing your view of men. We have to determine not to reject or become defensive because our husbands are different and will respond differently than us to a lot of situations.

Sexuality cannot be restored without allowing men to lead. God has divine order. A man in leadership is His order. If you reject this order, you repeatedly allow the theft of true sexuality in your life.

Coming into marriage, I had a disregard for authority. When Ray tried to lead, he was met with opposition because I felt like either I could do it better or his way was not the best way. Ray understood his God-given position to lead his family and I understood my need to "help" him lead this family. Any home with two leaders is a home divided. To restore sexuality, I had to give up my need to have control and trust God makes no mistakes and He had divinely given Ray to me.

Ray had no role models to teach him what authentic Christian leadership looked like and on many occasions, I saw his lack of immediate action as passivity. Whether our husbands are, in our opinions, equipped to lead or not, they are the leaders. To see your husband as leader and allow him to lead, you begin to restore your own sexuality.

Whether your husband knows how to lead, whether or not he is walking with God, whether he is passive or unsaved, he is still the leader in your home. The only time there should be an exception to his leadership if he is asking you to sin by going against God or His Word. This is how you can submit to him just as you would the Lord. Listen to God on this issue: Ephesians 5:22-24, "Wives, submit yourselves unto your own husbands, as unto the Lord. For the husband is the head of the wife, even as Christ is the head of the church; and he is the savior of the body. Therefore as the church is subject unto Christ, so let wives be to their own husbands in everything." (And for hard-heads like me who believe that the Lord didn't really mean what He said, He wrote it again in Colossians 3:18, Titus 2:5, 1 Peter 3:1, and 1 Peter 3:5.)

Half of your true sexuality will be restored by grasping who you are in all your femaleness. Your femaleness allows you to be all that God intended you to be when He created you as a helper. You are your husband's private personal assistant and if he doesn't look good, you have to look at yourself.

I once heard that the Hebrew word for helper means "rescuer." I wanted to rescue Ray long before he had cried out for help. Because of my intuition (and being a fast thinker and fast responder), I would try to rescue him and believed that he would continue to need me to rescue him. This caused me to think that Ray would need rescuing all of the time, stripping him of his opportunity to lead. And once I got myself out of the way, I found that

Ray is a great leader and I was preventing him from leading because I already had it figured out for the both of us.

The other half of your true sexuality will be restored by allowing your husband to be who he is created to be in all of his maleness. He is a leader! God gave us examples all through His Word of different kinds of leaders. How would you have liked to be Sarah when Abraham said, "we are moving and I don't know where we are going"? Most of us would say, "You go ahead and 'find yourself' and send for me when you are established." Or maybe be Lot's wife, submerged in a culture that both of you are content with and one day hear, "We have to leave and never look back!" Our husbands' leadership will never look like our leadership because (1) we are not supposed to be fighting him for the leadership role and (2) he is male and altogether different from female.

In order to restore your stolen sexuality, you must restore maleness and femaleness, masculinity and femininity, male and female back to God's divine order in creation.

Why the World Is Missing It

The entire Bible is true. In Ecclesiastes 1:9-10, it says, "What has happened before will happen again. What has been done before will be done again. There is nothing new in the whole world. 'Look' they say, 'here's something new!' but no, it has all happened before, long before we were born."

One of the many tactics that Satan uses to lie and steal from us is to take a truth from God and distort it. Satan has distorted the family. He tells us that a family is what we say a family is, and that there is no need for a mother, father, or children.

Satan has distorted our churches. He initiates compromise and the fall of leaders to make us believe God is not always present. Satan has distorted our focus. He makes us think that so many other things are important and turns our focus from God directing our paths. Satan has distorted sex. He has lied to us and told us that God's design of sex is not the only way to intimacy.

Every life has been touched with the distortion of Satan. Sexual intimacy and misdirected focus have been one of his most destructive tactics. There is nothing new under the sun. Satan has made the world believe that sexual intimacy can be attained outside of marriage.

God created sex, and sex, outside God's boundaries, is a blatant distortion of truth. This distortion leaves us with pain and causes us to guard our hearts. Our guarded hearts have stolen our sexuality right out from under us because Satan has taken the beauty of sex and made it a travesty. He has taken God's creation and made it an inferior imitation. He has masked it so that we think it is the real thing. Satan tells us that sex should be this passionate interlude with no commitment or connection.

That if "I" don't have an orgasm, if "I" don't feel like you deserve it, or if "I" am not in the mood, then "I" don't have to give sex. Because, after all, Satan has us believing that sex is all about "me."

But when we become aware we have been fooled, we become keenly aware of the pains we are left with. These pains include guilt, memories, shame, and deception. He continues to shame us into believing that because of our poor choices, we cannot share the truth with others coming behind us. "Who am I to talk?" was the reply of one of my girlfriends regarding her own sexual past.

I remember a colleague's openness about her conversation on sex with one of her daughters. She always made the subject of sex an open topic in their home and answered her children's questions honestly. She said, "They know when you are making it up. If you are not having a healthy relationship, you will not have a lot to say." This friend told me that she and her husband kept sex in high regard. Even by talking openly with their children, several did indeed fall prey to the distortion of the world and had pre-marital sex.

The world also tells you that if your husband is not giving, why should you? It teaches us that sex should be individually gratifying, and if he is not meeting your needs, why should you meet his? The world is teaching women and men that marital sex should be selfish—it is all about you.

The world tells you that because of all that you give, this should be one area that you don't have to give. The world has taken God's precious gift of sexual intimacy and tried to repackage it; offering it back to us, and we have chosen to accept it—hook, line, and sinker.

My Precious Gift Was Stolen from Me, and I Want It Back

Satan doesn't want you and your husbands' relationship to show God off. He has set his biggest, most violent, sure-to-kill attack on your intimacy. If Satan can get you to have intimacy issues with your husband who you can see, then he surely can get you to have intimacy issues with your Father in Heaven who you cannot see. "If anyone says, "I love God," yet hates his brother, he is a liar. For anyone who does not love his brother, whom he has seen, cannot love God, whom he has not seen" (John 4:20).

Having intimacy issues with your husband will cause you to doubt or lose faith in the one you are in relationship with. Having intimacy issues with the Father will cause you to lose faith in God. When this happens, Satan has accomplished his primary desire.

A healthy sexual relationship is a relationship where trust is absolute. Trust in sex is essential. To not have trust in sex will leave you feeling used. To feel used will set up self-preservation: the establishment of false intimacy. False intimacy takes you back to feeling like no one is trustworthy, and the cycle continues.

When I was a little girl, I began to distrust men. I felt the discipline of my father was often brought on by anger and was uncontrolled. I didn't understand some of the reasons we, as children, were being disciplined. I also feared the conflicts between my parents because objects would sometimes fly right above my head.

Outside the home, some of the male leaders in our church didn't act as though they had a personal relationship with Christ. As a teen, I began to fight with my father and it caused me to set up this false dependency in myself. Coming into marriage with Ray, this distrust was made more evident because I was becoming one with this man. As our lives began to weave together more and more, I knew I would have to come to terms with this distrust.

How did I get to a place where self-preservation was not my first instinct? Matthew 16:24-26 (Good News Translation) says, "Then Jesus said to his disciples, 'If anyone wants to come with me, he must forget self, carry his cross, and follow me. For whoever wants to save his own life will lose it; but whoever loses his life for my sake will find it. Will people gain anything if they win the whole world but lose their life? Of course not! There is nothing they can give to regain their life.'"

In order to get to the place where we are less concerned with self, and for the preservation of ourselves, we must make a deliberate choice to follow Christ's way. To deny self is to leave behind anything that puts your own needs over the obedience of following Christ. "Carry His cross" is used to illustrate that we will have afflictions and troubles that we must bear. Once again, hardships will touch every life.

If being sick of sex is your trouble, and you know that you are a believer in Christ, then Satan has waged war against your intimacy with your husband and with Christ. It is the cross you must carry. If you continue in the self-preservation mode, you will end up losing your life. You will lose the abundant life that God has planned for you, and you will live a mediocre life of existence. You will lose all that is important, and you will lose your intimate relationship with your husband. At the end of your life, you may think you preserved yourself, but true intimacy was forfeited.

By losing your life and following Christ, you find your true life. And in your true life, sexual intimacy is trusted and peaceful.

> *I am crucified with Christ: nevertheless I live, yet not I, but Christ liveth in me: and the life which I now live in the flesh I live by the faith of the Son of God, who loved me, and gave himself for me. — (Galatians 2:20)*

JOURVOTIONAL

Stealing Our Sexuality

1. How did your mother (or any female adult in your life) prepare you for a godly sexual relationship in marriage?

_____

_____

_____

2. What are some of the "secret code names" you have heard sex referred to as?

_____

_____

3. If you are a mom, what are some ways you are preparing your own children for a godly sexual relationship?

_____

_____

_____

4. Write out four things you wish you had been told about a healthy sexual relationship before you were married?

_____

_____

_____

_____

5. How was masculinity and femininity modeled for you in your early years?

_____

_____

6. Who were your godly role models growing up? Your husband's?

_____

_____

7. Why were you attracted to the godly role models?

_____

_____

8. Who are the friends with whom you can openly talk to about sex?

_____

_____

9. Who are the friends who will talk to you about sex?

_____

_____

10. What are the ways you see self-preservation creeping into your marriage?

_____

_____

_____

_____

Simple Ways to Begin Restoring Your Sexuality

1. When your children ask, give them a Godly view of sexual intimacy.

2. Watch a family movie together and begin having discussions about the ethics of this movie. What was wrong (principles that are not Biblical) about the movie? What are Godly principles of this movie?

3. Pray with your family. Pray that God will restore some of the things that Satan has stolen or has tried to steal from you.

S.O.S. — CHAPTER #18

SEARCH OUT SANCTUARIES

Now be ye not stiff necked, as your fathers were, but yield yourselves unto the LORD, and enter into his sanctuary, which he hath sanctified forever. — (2 Chronicles 30:8)

The single most important step to becoming a woman who lays down the S.O.S. of being sick of sex begins here. You must search out sanctuaries. A sanctuary is a safe place where you are protected and energized to get back into the fight and fight to win. Your sanctuary must include time alone where you can personally be invigorated to do all that is required of you.

Times of sanctuary will never come easy. There will always be things that stand in your way to make sanctuary time difficult. Satan will make sure these times are hard to have because he knows how sanctuary time will fuel you towards true intimacy with your husband and with Christ. Not having times of sanctuary is a silent S.O.S. cry. Your sanctuary time is your salvation in your desperate cry for healing. Your search for sanctuary will lead you on a quest for intimacy. As you search out sanctuaries, you will find true intimacy.

In order to begin your search for these sanctuaries, you must know what kind of sanctuary you are looking for. I believe there have to be at least three sanctuaries that need to be regular (scheduled and kept) in every Christian marriage.

They are:

1. Your home as a sanctuary
2. A time away from home
3. Personal sanctuary

Your Home as a Sanctuary

Everyone who has a home should feel that their home is a safe place. If you work outside your home, you should look forward to arriving home to a place of sanctuary. Your home should be a place of refuge where you are energized (fueled) to go on. When your husband leaves for his job, he should look forward to coming home. He wants to be met with a wife who respects and loves him and children who think he is "all that and a bag of chips."

In the Tyndale Bible Dictionary, sanctuary refers to the place where God appeared and/or dwelt (as indicated by the presence of the ark). Tyndale goes on to say that God's Word was kept there and issued forth from it. It was the place where God's people gathered for sacrifice, hearing the covenant Word, worship, prayer, and for the celebration of the major feasts.

Your sanctuary time is your salvation in your desperate cry for healing.

Ask yourself these questions: Does my home feel like a place of sanctuary? Is it a place where God's Word is kept and the commandments of His Word are issued forth? Is it a place where other Christians want to gather?

Harper's Bible Dictionary says that a sanctuary is "the holy place where Hebrews believed the Lord was present." When you are in your home, do you feel the presence of the Lord?

If you and your husband have intimacy issues and they go unaddressed, the presence of the Lord will not be felt in your home. There is something about intimacy; it cannot be faked for long. If your home is not a sanctuary, you will not feel safe to begin to address the intimacy issues. When intimacy is missing, a home does not feel like a sanctuary to those who enter. It especially does not feel like a sanctuary to those who live there. A home that is missing sanctuary is a home where no one wants to hang out. You, your husband, or your children find reasons not to be home.

Children love places that register as a "safe haven" to them. Oh, they also love a place that has the latest and greatest toys, but even the toys, without sanctuary, aren't enough for children to stay. If your children always want to go over someone else's home and never invite others to your house, then you have to question their eagerness to get away. We need to look at our homes and see if we are providing a safe haven or if we are "tearing down with our own hands" (Proverbs 14:1).

A Time Away from Home

Even if your home is a safe haven, it is necessary to get away (vacate) periodically.

Growing up in the Holiness church, at the end of each service there was an altar call. This altar call was a serious time. It was a time where you would come forward and lay your burdens down, symbolically, at the foot of the cross. The choir usually sang, "Is Your All on the Altar?" or "I Surrender All." The pastor would say Hebrews 4:16, "Let us then with confidence draw near to the throne of grace that we may receive mercy and find grace to help in time of need." To kneel at the altar, you experienced a time of sanctuary with the Lord and when you got up from that time of intimate prayer, you were energized. You had the strength to make it.

In order to have a sanctuary in your home, you must have a time where you have an "altar call" with your husband, a time where you lay your marriage down at the foot of the cross so God can give you the strength to get up and fight the battles that will come after your intimacy.

There are many of us who have never spent any length of time away with only our husbands. Most of us are committed to having an occasional date so we can stay connected, but dates just aren't enough. Ray and I find ourselves talking more about the kids on dates than we talk about our own relationship.

There are just some things in life that are worth the investment. Take a car, for example. In order for it to continue to drive from point A to point B, we have to make an investment in gas. As close to that 3,000-mile mark as possible, we get an oil change. Every two years or 30,000 miles, we make sure to get a tune-up. Even the owner's manual tells us that we need this major service so our car stays functional. On occasion, there comes a time when the car has a serious problem. We take it to the service technician and he tells us we must take care of a certain issue with the car so it will not break down. So, we wisely make an appointment for the repair.

Our desire is to have the car in and out of the shop quickly. We want same day service. But there are some issues that keep us from getting our car back the same day. The mechanic must keep the car overnight to assess what is wrong or to get the appropriate part. We ask the technician how much we think that this little overnight fix is going to cost us, and he gives us an astronomical number; we protest. He then states that we can either fix the car the right way, now, or wait until the car breaks down and have it towed to get the same fix. We swallow hard and then tell him, "fix the car."

We make all the necessary adjustments to our family and work schedules so we can have a trustworthy car. Our car is trustworthy because we take the time for a mechanic to look at it when we deem something is wrong, but our marriages are breaking down all over the place. Our marriages need to have a greater priority than our cars. We want a relationship with our husband that is trustworthy. So, we need to make sure we have the periodic oil changes. These are dinner and lunch dates.

But in every marriage, there comes a time when we need "major service." This major service prevents the marriage from breaking down on us. It needs to be a time where we go away from all that is familiar. We need to make the necessary adjustments with our family and work schedules to get away. This investment will take money you might not have to spare, but just like your car, we need to make the investment to have that marriage tune-up. Often times, we take our marriages for granted and forget to have these tune-ups. But, just as any other thing that you want to keep, you must take care of it along the way. Maintenance maintains.

A car that hasn't had an oil change knocks and ticks. The car lets you know that an oil change is overdue, and the knocking and ticking gets louder until that oil gets changed, or until the car breaks down.

Our un-tuned marriages knock and tick. To you, your husband, and all who are around, it does not ride smoothly. Everyone can hear the knocking and ticking, and realizes the ride is not as smooth as it should be. The longer we wait to tune-up, the louder the knocking and ticking. We think we are going through a rough spot and it, too, will pass. But just as with your car, it won't pass until you take time to address what is wrong. This knocking and ticking reveals a dirty and clogged relationship. Unattended, just as a car without an oil change, the pressure of the unlubricated engine will cause major damage. It may even take a serious monetary investment.

If your car breaks down, what measures would you take to get it repaired? What about your marriage?

Over the years as a pastor's wife, I have seen people go to others to borrow money to get their car repaired. I have seen them go to other couples in the church and even to the church's benevolence fund. But how many of us will go to a couple at church or the church, itself, and ask them to make an investment in our breaking-down marriage? Marriage upkeep is far more important than the upkeep of anything you think is necessary for life's comfort.

Our culture tells us that just when your car breaks down and it is too expensive to repair, go buy a new model. That is what we are doing with our marriages. We are throwing out what we deem too expensive of our time and finances to repair, and we get a new model—only to find out that the new model requires the same investment and maintenance as the old one.

Satan is looking for a marriage he can devour. We are being eaten up by the enemy of marriage because we have allowed him to throw a wrench into our marriage and we have not taken the necessary time to remove it.

We must search out sanctuaries for our marriages. We must invest time and resources in our marriages. We absolutely have to look for places where we can get away.

Invest more than an occasional meal and two hours of paying a babysitter and make necessary fixes to your marriage. Sanctuary time will be marriage retreats, conferences, and get-a-ways where you can get into God's Word because His Word "Is breathed out by God and profitable for teaching, for reproof, for correction, and for training in righteousness, that the man of God may be competent, equipped for every good work" (2 Timothy 3:16). This is what sanctuary time will do for you. These opportunities give you a chance to look at your marriage and see all the wrenches inside of it and what has got to go for it to run smoothly.

Now with the busyness of life, we have placed the necessary tune-ups on the back burner. We say to ourselves, "We will have more time and money next year to spend on each other," or "once the kids are gone." But in order to have intimacy, you must spend intimate, exclusive time together now. And that is an investment that cannot wait on money or an empty house.

When Ray and I first married, we were blessed with Raychel ten months after our wedding. We were living life with all the responsibility of a new house payment, a new baby, and both our jobs. I was surprised when Ray walked in one day and said he had signed us up to go to a FamilyLife marriage conference. We were BROKE! How in the world could we squeeze anything more out of our budget? But one of my sisters agreed to keep Raychel and we left for the conference.

The conference made us dig deep, and we ended up dealing with a lot of stuff we had ignored. We cried, (or should I say, I cried, and Ray pouted). But it made us talk about our relationship. It made us deal with the not-so-pleasant so we could get to the pleasant. It made us tune-up our relationship.

Every marriage needs a time of outside sanctuary. This sanctuary has to be a consecrated place, a place of refuge and protection. The only way this sanctuary works is if the center of it provides you with an altar to lay your marriage upon. This altar is the place where you offer your marriage back to the One who gave it to you. The altar is where the blemishes and wrinkles are ironed out so you go home with a new perspective. This new attitude provides you with the wisdom and grace to establish a home that is a sanctuary.

> *The only thing that will keep you wanting to invest in your marriage is to invest in yourself.*

The Personal Sanctuary

The only thing that will keep you wanting to invest in your marriage is to invest in yourself. You must have daily, personal times of sanctuary. Abraham could trust God to take him where "I will show you" (Genesis 12:1), because he had a personal relationship with God. Abraham trusted God because he knew God was trustworthy. In Genesis 19:27, Abraham, "got up early in the morning to the place where he stood before the Lord." There is no way he would be able to trust God blindly without times of personal sanctuary.

Your marriage is unique. To attain a godly marriage, you must have times of personal sanctuary. The only way Moses could feel powerful enough to go before Pharaoh was because of his time of personal sanctuary. Moses, together with his brother, Aaron, freed millions of Jewish people. In Exodus 6:28-7:2, "On the day when the Lord spoke to Moses in the land of Egypt, the Lord said to Moses, 'I am the Lord: tell Pharaoh King of Egypt all that I say to you.'"

How can you fight what is so powerfully strong against your marriage without personal sanctuary? Your personal sanctuary will give you the power (energy) to free your marriage from the grips of the enemy. This time of personal sanctuary is the time that you spend tuning-up your life with God so you can hear His voice, and He can direct your path. This is your daily quiet time where you surrender your will to His. (This does not have to be a formal Bible study, just time with you and God, no matter how long.)

We all have to have sanctuaries in our lives. They will not be easy to attain or maintain. Everything in this world would have you dismiss these times, but you must fight to have them. They have to be kept and never disregarded.

A disregarded personal life is engine failure waiting to happen. A non-prioritized marriage is an immobilized car. And a home that is not a sanctuary is the car with no working engine. Useless.

> *"You keep him in perfect peace who mind is stayed on you, because he trusts in you. Trust in the Lord forever, for the Lord God is an everlasting rock."* — (Isaiah 26:3-4)

JOURVOTIONAL

Search Out Sanctuaries

1. When is the last time, and at what place, did you find sanctuary where you were able to be refueled?

_____

2. Does your home feel like a place of sanctuary? _____

Is it a place where God's Word is kept and the commandments of His Word are issued forth? _____

Is it a place where other Christians want to gather? _____

3. When and where was the last get-away with your husband? _____

Did you address the state of your marriage and intimacy?

_____

4. What are some measures you are taking to make sure your marriage stays well-tuned and without major repair?

_____

_____

_____

_____

5. Do you have a personal time of sanctuary? If so, specifically what does this time look like? If not, what would a personal time of sanctuary look like in your mind?

_____

_____

_____

6. Read again Isaiah 26:3-4. What is God telling you, personally, in this verse of scripture?

_____

_____

_____

7. Spend time in prayer. Use this time as a personal sanctuary time for your own personal refreshment with the Lord.

S.O.S. — CHAPTER #19

SOLD OUT SISTER

Two are better than one… For if they fall, the one will lift up his fellow: but woe to him that is alone when he falls; for he has not another to lift him up. — (Ecclesiastes 4:9-10)

I have 5 sisters: 4 biological and 1 adopted sister who I know will always tell me the truth. Whether the truth is what I want to hear or not, they are sometimes brutally honest. Their honesty will never change our relationship because no matter what they say to me, nothing will change the fact that we have the same mother and father. If I decide that I no longer want to have anything to do with them, even legally change my name, the DNA that flows through our blood can never be changed.

My sisters normally tell me the truth because they are more concerned with my well-being (or with me hearing their opinion) than how I may respond to what is being said. They tell me the truth because they know that even though they might be hurting me now, they believe that they will be helping me in the long run. Often times, our relationship may be strained for a while, but in the end, I know, Carolyn, Gail, Debra, Stephanie, and Vanessa will always be my sisters.

But even with my sisters, I find myself running from the relationship if it becomes too difficult. Keeping the lines of communication open has not always been easy but we understand that it is imperative. There have been times that I have intentionally been busy when one of them calls, taking my time to return a call, avoiding them or having strained conversation.

Satan has us on a road where we run away from any-thing that seems too difficult for us. We run away from most relationships that could cause us discomfort. We are running so much that it is hindering us from listening, learning, and growing. When we run for the human relationships that we are a part of, we run away from God when the road He is taking us down doesn't seem comfortable or safe.

When my girlfriends or sisters say anything I dislike or disagree with, it seems easier to be guarded in this relationship or move on to another friendship. It makes me determine to never be so vulnerable the next time. I, in turn, place an unwanted shield around my heart. Satan wants us to believe that relationships are too risky.

When we run away by ourselves with no help in getting to our destination, we usually run down the wrong path and need directions. Having sold out sisters in your life is like having an extra compass when you are broken down on the highway of life.

We need a sister or friend who has nothing to lose with us.

We need a sister or friend who has nothing to lose with us. She needs to be someone who is more concerned with what the Lord thinks of what she says than what we think of what she says. We need a sister who knows that nothing in this world will change the fact that both of you have been adopted into the family of God, and that once you are in, there is no way to get out. She is sold out to the Lord and she understands that her words are not her own. She has been bought with a price and she must represent her ownership.

Your sold out sister understands that your relationship with her is not "until death do you part" but it is eternally forever. No matter what she says to you, she will be with you in Heaven and her exhortations now will not at all affect your relationship there. We need sold out sisters to always point us back to the Lord and His ways. No matter how difficult God's way may seem. No matter if it feels right to us. Once again, God's ways are not like our ways.

Sold Out "Older" Sisters

It is a command that older women are to teach younger women to love their husbands (Titus 2:3-4). Another factor in our becoming sick of sex is we don't have older women available who will address sexual intimacy. Our churches are filled with women who don't even know what is going on sexually in the lives of their best girlfriends. I don't believe we should go into the most intimate details of our sex lives with our best friends, but we need to have accountability in this area, too. Marriage should include an active sexual relationship, and we need those around us who are trustworthy and who we are accountable to, and they to us. We are living in our churches like we do in our neighborhoods. We drive in and shut the garage door. We only come outside to get the mail, and if we run into a neighbor, we surface talk. God's house should be a place of safety and security where conversation should build us up. But even in our churches, we don't have real relationships.

God never intended for us to be in relationship with anyone to just surface talk. Surface talk should be used as a tool to take us into deeper communication with those who become a part of our inner circle. We then move from surface talk to authentic communication. This communication is so real that it is refreshing and breathes life into you.

I imagine sitting in a corner stall of a restaurant restroom when a new mom entered with her crying baby. As this new mom lowered the changing station, I see an older woman enter the restroom. She is wearing a "Jesus Saves" pin and carrying a Bible as if she had just come from church. Now the young mom and her newborn baby were both crying.

The older woman noticed that this new mom was having difficulty changing the baby's diaper, and the baby was having a fit. The baby had pooped up its back and all over the mom. She noticed the frustration and immediately came to her aid. The diaper was changed by the older mom, while the new mom cleaned herself up as best as possible. The crying had stopped and the older woman held tightly to this new mom as she clung to her calming baby.

This story is God's command. Regrettably, we don't always help the new moms because we've got to go to the

restroom and our need to relieve ourselves is more press-
ing than the need to mentor. We have been taught that
other people's business is their own, and we are safe if we
just stay out of it. You might even think to yourself, "She
needs to learn to change her own baby's diapers, anyways." But we must learn and understand that there is
safety in numbers. We are never safe alone. God tells us
in Proverbs 11:14, "where there is no guidance, a people
falls, but in an abundance of counselors there is safety."

We are sending an S.O.S. cry out, begging our
Heavenly Father for women who can help us along in our
journey. God can and has provided sold out sisters to
bring us safety. We not only need one sold out sister, we
need many of these godly counselors who will offer us
truth.

In our lives, we need sold out sisters who will be comfortable asking us about our intimate relationship with
our husbands and with Christ. We need women in our
lives that are close enough with us to give us an accurate
description of where we truly are. These are women who
allow you to tell the truth instead of hide it. These are
women who don't want the details of your sexual experience with your husband but they want to know where
your intimacy is.

We live by the commands of God that we deem
important, but older women teaching younger women
seems to be optional. This mentoring of younger women

is happening on a large scale in some of our churches but there are so many women who desire to have a woman walk beside them and there are none found. (While speaking at a conference I asked the 300 ladies in attendance, "who has an older women investing in your life?" More than half of the ladies didn't have any kind of relationship like this.) I believe we think the younger women have it all together, and older women are thinking, "Since my nest is empty, I will now be able to accomplish some of the things I've always wanted to do." So the investment in the lives of those coming behind us is rarely taking place.

There is a generation gap in our culture that keeps older women and younger women feeling as if there is nothing there to build a connection. Both older and younger women have a lot to learn from each other. Older women have so much to offer younger women and younger women have such need for experience and wisdom. This gap continues to grow larger because of misunderstanding in our communication. Here's another truth that my momma used to say all the time, and now that I have lived quite a few years, I understand: "It's not what you say, it's how you say it."

Ray and I had our first two babies very quickly. We celebrated our second anniversary three days after our second child was born. Shortly thereafter, I had another positive pregnancy test. I proudly told the ladies in the choir at our church one Wednesday night at rehearsal that we were soon to be parents again. The very next Friday, I miscarried. I moped around all day Friday and Saturday. On Sunday morning, I got up and dressed for church. Ray encouraged me to take another day of rest and stay home but I wanted to be around people. So, still feeling a little "blue," I knew I would be lifted up at church. After getting my two little ones settled, I took my position at the piano and had a wonderful time of worship and praise. God's Word in that Sunday morning sermon was just what I needed.

There was this older woman in the choir; I had really taken a liking to her. When she sang, you could close your eyes and experience a little taste of the music of Heaven. While I was playing the benediction hymn, she came over and sat by me on the piano bench. As soon as the song was over, she gave me a big hug and some of her wisdom: "Robyn, I am so sorry about your miscarriage, but, God never intended for us to breed like dogs." This older woman got up from the piano bench and began greeting other saints. I was left at that bench, tears streaming, and feeling even more down than when I first entered the service.

I loved this woman. I wish she would have known how to politely tell me she was concerned for my health and that she maybe thought I was, in her opinion, delivering babies too quickly. As younger women, we absolutely need older women in our lives but if someone says something that offends you, you must not retreat. We need these women; their wisdom and experience is invaluable for our Christian growth. If someone hurts our feelings by something they've said, we need to analyze what they are saying and why they are saying it. We need to continue communicating with them because we shape and sharpen each other. We must begin honest communication by letting her know that what she said was offensive. (Matthew 18:15)

As older women, we cannot be intimated by younger women, but we have to develop skills that allow us to be heard by them. This skill development is cultivated by an investment of time and attention to them. Build a rapport with someone and you capture their attention and trust. But we are often rushed by time so we bluntly tell them "our truth." We, as older women, need to be women of God's Word. We need to build our bias and convictions on the Word. We need to be women who can be looked to not because we are fashionable, but because we are fashioned after God. Younger women need to be encouraged in God's Word with the truth, not just our version of it. We must absolutely learn to speak the truth of God's Word…in love.

There are reasons all this mentoring in the church has not produced encouraged women or godly families. We have a few women and families that stand the test of time, but most are passing by the wayside, living mediocre Christian lives and often producing lost and hurt off-spring. Sold out sisters must pass on godly wisdom because they are walking in the Spirit of God.

The Bible clearly lays out the kind of women we should look for when we want someone to input into our lives. Titus 2:3-5 says, "Older women likewise are to be reverent in behavior, not slanderers or slaves to much wine. They are to teach what is good, and so train young women to love their husbands and children, to be self-controlled, pure, working at home, kind and submissive to their own, husbands, that the word of God may not be reviled."

Too many of us are looking for a woman who we think has it all together, knows plenty of scripture, and can pray down Heaven. But are we looking for women who are reverent in behavior because they love their husbands and children? Are they reverent because God's Word tells them to be and that alone would be enough for their obedience? Are they self-controlled, pure, prioritizing home, kind, and submissive to their own husbands?

For just a quick moment, I would like for you to return to fifth-grade English with me. We need to review synonyms and antonyms. A synonym is a word you can use in place of another word, and it has the same meaning but gives another picture of that word. Antonyms are the exact opposite of the word you are trying to describe.

When you think of the word *authentic*, what would be some synonyms for this word? Synonyms are: *genuine, real, valid, bona fide, true, reliable,* and *dependable*. Now think of all the things that you own that you know are authentic. Some would be your marriage, your wedding ring, money in your pocket, your name, and your salvation.

Now let's look at antonyms for the word *authentic*. We need only one, *fake*. Let's say, one day, you woke to find that all the things in your life that your thought was authentic were actually fake. We may think there would be nothing to live for. We need to follow after genuine, bona fide, true, reliable, dependable role models and not fake ones.

There are some of you who are reading this book and the sexual experience, for you, has been one that you'd rather not talk about. You have already raised your children and are wondering what to do in the retirement years. I believe God has called you to be an investor—not of your financial wealth, but of your life's wisdom.

There are many young women out there who need someone to invest in their lives. They need some surrogate mothers and grandmothers. These women don't really care if you can quote a scripture from the Bible or tell them where it is found, they just need you!

We are sick of sex because our sold out "older" sisters shy away, not wanting to admit their own issues in this area. But when you invest your life, the advice and counsel you give to others has a way of affecting life change for you.

When I was a little girl, I thought my momma was the best thing going. Better than cake and ice cream. Today, I am a mother of five girls and four boys, and I realize there are a few things Momma forgot to tell, teach, and model for me. I know that my momma did her best with what she knew and understood. There were just some crucial areas that were left with gaps.

Today, I know how to praise God for the gaps. If Momma had done mothering perfectly, I would have no reason to go before the Lord and ask for His wisdom and help. It would be my first inclination to go to Momma.

We need sold out sisters in our lives because no momma will ever do all that there is to mothering right. How blessed I am to have others who desire to walk with the Lord who can help fill in the gaps. But our gaps will never be completely filled by the women in our lives. These are just gap-filler-helpers…if they point us to God, our gaps will be completely filled by Him.

My mom had girlfriends who were Christian ladies, and I spent my time with the children of her girlfriends. I was around Christian women all the time, and they were able to fill some of my missing gap areas. I have Christian friends who my own children feel the freedom to call for their opinions and advise. These women are helping to fill in the gaps for my children.

We need sold out sisters who are gap fillers. We will never be a perfect wife or perfect mother. Have ladies in your life that will help you to fill the gaps that we all have. These gaps keep us "at the foot of the cross," knowing that Luke 18:27 is true, "But, he said, "What is impossible with men is possible with God." The godly gap fillers will lift you up and let you know that being sick of sex is impossible to alleviate alone but is possible with God.

Sold Out "Peer" Sisters

We need sisters that are sold out to the Lord that are in the same age group, stage of life or similar situation (married, working outside the home, homemaker, children, or no children etc.) as we are. Some of these sold out sisters will not fit the mold of what we think we may need. One of my dearest peer sold out sisters is a friend of mine who doesn't mind telling me the truth.

You never have to guess where you stand with her. She is extremely honest so, if you don't want the truth, don't ask for her opinion. The sweet thing about her is that her honesty never comes across as critical. She genuinely gives her opinion, and she also calls for my honest opinion in return.

We, as a nation of Christian women, are praying for honest friends. Christian women need honest friends in our lives. Sadly, we have pushed away those with this quality because we don't want anyone to know or point out our sin areas. Having honest friends in your life, no matter how rare they may be, help make you an authentic person. You will begin to look at life honestly and respond to life's situations honestly.

We need those in the same stage of life that we are in. It would be difficult to talk about sexual things with a woman whose eighty-year-old husband is struggling with impotence if we are in our twenties or thirties. When it comes to our sex lives, we need honesty. We need a friend who will tell us the truth, who we know will not judge us but point us to all God has intended for us and our husband.

Even though Elizabeth was older, when Mary knew she was pregnant, she had a cousin who was in the same stage of life. Pregnant together, Elizabeth is able to validate what God has told Mary. Luke 1:41-43, "And when Elizabeth heard the greeting of Mary, the baby leaped in her womb. And Elizabeth was filled with the Holy Spirit, and she exclaimed with a loud cry, "Blessed are you among women, and blessed is the fruit of your womb! And why is this granted to me that the mother of my Lord should come to me?" Mary stays with Elizabeth about three months for encouragement.

Sold out "peer" sisters are able to walk with you through tough things that haven't been so far removed from their own paths. These women are, on occasion, painfully honest but wanting God's best for you.

You Are a Sold Out Sister

Women need women. The neat thing about God is that He placed enough women on Earth to be able to help other women. There is no shortage of women, but there is a great shortage of investors. Whether we know it or not, there are younger women, friends, and older women who are looking at us for inspiration to see how we do what we do. There is a woman out there who needs you to be her sold out sister, one who she can depend on to tell her the truth of God's Word rather than what she may want to hear.

In Romans 12:3-6 we are told: "For by the grace given to me I say to everyone among you not to think of himself more highly that he ought to think, but to think with sober judgment, each according to the measure of faith that God has assigned. For as in one body we have many members, and the members do not all have the same function, so we, though many, are one body in Christ, and individually members one of another. Having gifts that differ according to the grace given to us, let us use them." God shows us that He has uniquely gifted us to be used in the body of Christ.

Investing in the lives of women takes work. It will take time, and it will take grace, all of which you will only receive supernaturally. God will have to give you the strength, availability, and grace to do the work. And He is not in short supply of any of it!

Again, if two lie together, they keep warm, but how can one keep warm along? And though a many might prevail against one who is alone, two will withstand him—a threefold cord is not quickly broken. — (Ecclesiastes 4:11-12)

JOURVOTIONAL

Sold Out Sister

1. Who is the one person in your life who is always free to give their opinion? _____

Do you tend to avoid their advice or accept it? Why?

_____

_____

2. List the mentors you have had over the course of your life—the women you have, at one time or another, wanted to pattern your life after.

_____

_____

_____

3. What has been one uncomfortable thing that a sold out sister has brought to your attention that has made you a more godly woman?

_____

_____

_____

_____

4. Right now, who is your mentor? _____

If you don't have one, name a woman who you would like to invest in your life. _____

5. Name 3 (three) female peers in your life who are in your same stage of life. _____,

_____, _____

6. Why are you attracted to these ladies?

_____

_____

_____

_____

_____

_____

7. Whose lives are you intentionally investing in?

_____

_____

_____

_____

8. What are some things you would want the person you are investing in to avoid?

_____

_____

_____

_____

_____

9. Read Ecclesiastes 4:11-12 again. Write in your own words what this means to you.

_____

_____

_____

_____

_____

10. Spend time alone, praying to God about the relationships you have with women or lack thereof. Write out

some things you would desire as a result of women's relationships in each other lives.

_____

_____

_____

_____

_____

Simple Ways to Find a Soul Out Sister

1. Get involved in your local church's women's ministry. Stay around after each event and strike up conversations with women you regularly see.

2. Sign up to take meals to homes that need them. Allow yourself extra time and get to know the lady of that house. (you can also do this by taking cookies to local nursing homes)

3. Pray and ask God to give you and the women around you boldness to see the need for women connecting.

4. Have a small women's game night, at your home, where getting to know each other is the main goal of the evening.

S.O.S. — CHAPTER #20

SUPER OFTEN SEX

*Do not deprive one another, except perhaps
by agreement for a limited time, that you
may devote yourselves to prayer; but then
come together again, so that Satan may not*

tempt you because of your lack of self-control. — (1 Corinthians 7:5)

The title of this chapter alone will get me bonus points with every married man on the planet. Our culture tells us that men want sex, often. But this chapter outlines the reason both men and women should desire sexual intimacy often, and it has nothing at all to do with the word "orgasm."

Many chapters in this book illustrate ways that Satan is lying to us in the area of sexual intimacy. God created sex and it is good. But you have to forsake (give up, renounce, turn your back on), the lies that Satan has used to destroy your sexual intimacy. The direct result of forsaking the lies of Satan, and knowing God's view of sex, is a relationship with your husband that includes super often sex. This is the timeless result of leaving sick of sex behind.

Super sex gives honor to God, because it is selfless sex. Your sexual intimacy will have no sin or guilt at all. You will desire to be with your husband and the outpouring of your intimate interaction will show the world who God is. Sex happens often when you see it as one of the best gifts that God has given to you. You will want to protect, maintain, and multiply this divine and intimate love.

Often, means "at short intervals or repeatedly." Our devotion to God doesn't get stale because we make sure we connect with Him "at short intervals or repeatedly." A relationship with God becomes stale when you don't meet with Him often. This is evidenced, over time, to all those around you. The same word, "often," should describe our sex lives when we desire our marriage to stay fresh and not go stale. Thus, a marriage becomes stale when sex is not often and is witnessed decreasing over time, by our family, friends, and children. This lack of intimacy that you first tried to hide is not only revealed but magnified.

Sex happens often when you see it as one of the best gifts that God has given to you.

Realistically, there will be times (seasons of sex) where mentally, physically, or spiritually sex is not as frequent as at other times. But as you yield to God, walking through this season, the result should be that you and your husband desire being together, often, once again.

I love to plant. I love gardens, houseplants, flowers, and greenery. My father taught me that plants don't grow without fertile ground. You have to prepare the ground, place the seeds in, watch so the birds don't steal your seeds, and wait for the plant to bloom and grow. Preparing the ground takes hard work, you have to turn over the soil to see what is there that would prevent the plant from springing up. This is all preparation for growth.

In the same way, we must prepare our hearts so sexual intimacy can bloom and grow. Much of what you have read is turning over the soil of your heart and preparing it for the newly planted seeds to take root and spring forth new life.

In order to prepare your heart for a dynamic sexual relationship, you have to have a relationship with the Lord where you are willing to surrender the areas that are not causing a fertile heart where God can move you from a mediocre intimacy to a supernatural one. God desires to give to His children. He desires that His children walk in truth. You are His child, and He will freely give every good thing to you, if you ask.

Picking Up the New Habits

We are creatures of habit. When something new is presented to us, we usually fall back into what is habitual for us unless we purposefully pick up the new. Seeing things in a new light dispels the old way we viewed them.

I was a nail biter. Until I was eighteen years old, I tried to stop biting my nails but found myself with my finger in my mouth and the nail down to a nub. Now more than thirty years later, I don't think about biting my nails at all. After eighteen years, I daily replaced the old nail biter with the new non-nail biter. To look at me today, you would never know I had an issue with biting nails.

For three years in high school I had terrible fights with my father. Even though they were few (maybe 8

317

fights), deep inside I felt I could never trust men and needed to depend on myself. I picked up a horrible habit of self-dependence.

Even after over twenty years of marriage, whenever I have a problem with Ray, which of these "habits" do you think is easier for me to fall back into nail biting or self-dependence? I put up my guard and fall back on self-dependency and self-preservation every time. I have never once thought about biting my nails even though I was a nail biter fourteen years longer. Satan was setting me up to die and go to Heaven with long, beautiful nails, a defunct marriage, and a messed up legacy.

There are some habits you have overcome that you will never pick up again. There are those who will never steal, lie, bite nails, abort children, date a married man, be anorexic, or bulimic, ever again. But with some of our reservations about sex, intimacy, trust, and dependence, we revert to old intimacy-robbing habits over and over again. We say we are going to trust God, knowing that He breaks bondages, but we find ourselves continually picking back up our old system of doubt.

Sexual intimacy is at the core of every marriage. Sex is withheld when the marriage is strained and sex is freely given if the marriage is good. Even though many have a good marriage, if sex is non-existent or rarely initiated, than the good marriage is a façade. We are not dealing with the thing or things that are hindering our intimacy.

Sex is at the core of marriage because growing in intimacy should be at the core of every marriage.

To maintain your relationship where super, often sex is supreme, you cannot fall back into what is habitual for you. The enemy of intimacy doesn't care about my bitten nails, but he is elated to see my distrust and selfish nature arising. My natural tendency to mistrust Ray because of my response to a bad situation long ago could keep me bound. But Jesus came to set captives free. I begin my freedom by obeying God's Word in 2 Corinthians 10:5-6, "We destroy arguments and every lofty opinion raised against the knowledge of God, and take every thought captive to obey Christ, being ready to punish every disobedience, when your obedience is complete."

As women, we have overcome many things. Yet, Satan continues to have us focus on what we have already attained instead of allowing our eyes to gaze on what God still has in store for us. Satan wants us to remain in captivity so he offers us victories that wane in comparison to what God has for us. Satan is saying, "Great job! You haven't bitten your nails in over twenty-eight years. Look what you have done!" God says, "Baby girl, love the nails, but I have a wonderful plan for your life with Ray, my precious gift to you."

Christ wants your natural inclination to be a godly response to life. He has the power to take your natural responses and make them supernatural. God wants you to offer the gift of sexual intimacy to your husband in a way that brings honor and glory to Him.

There is a song that I had been singing for years and loved it. It says, "Holiness, Holiness is what I long for. Holiness is what I need. Holiness, Holiness is what you want from me." I passionately sang this song for all those years grateful that the Lord of my Heart wants Holiness from me. But the other day, I was riding in my car and I heard an artist sing this same song. I chimed in with exuberance, singing over her. As I sang, I noticed she had changed one little word. Instead of saying Holiness is what you want FROM me, she used the phrase, "Holiness, Holiness is what you want FOR me." That little word change brought happy tears to my eyes.

God wants you to offer the gift of sexual intimacy to your husband in a way that brings honor and glory to Him.

God created intimacy "for" us. He didn't create intimacy for us to believe that it is what our husbands want "from," us. This revelation changes our whole reason for intimacy. Too many of us view sexual intimacy as something our husbands need. When we are fatigued or have strained relationships, his desire for intimacy is one more thing we have to give. We are constantly giving throughout the day and to give him sex is another form of work. But if we view sexual intimacy as a gift *from* God *for* us, it changes the very essence of intimacy.

Do you want a healthy sexual relationship? Ask for it. Ask your Father in Heaven because He has already created it *for you.*

It would be very easy to do everything in this book and find yourself right back in the same old rut in a couple of months. But it doesn't have to be that way.

> You can set your stage by de-cluttering your mind, attitude, and schedule.

> You can come to terms with the unique body that God has given you.

> You can learn the art of sensuality, the added bonus to intimacy.

> You can learn to view sex through different eyes and see that God has set it apart.

> You can even wake up one day next to the most sensitive man you know, and you can't image life without him.

> You can change your view of sex and learn its purpose.

> You can die to yourself and selfishness, daily.

> You can learn to find safety in the arms of
> your husband and regain your sexuality.

All of these things are stepping stones to get you to the place where you believe that God did create intimacy *for* us. It is one of His good and perfect gifts. (James 1:17) He never intended it to be something we have to grudgingly give because we are tired, have issues with our husbands, or even issues with ourselves. It is *for* us so we experience intimacy with our husbands, giving us a little of the intimacy we will share with Christ when we are in Heaven. That's right. Sexual intimacy with your husband is a precursor to the intimacy we will have with Christ ... our Bridegroom. That intimate relationship between two people with no deception, no selfishness, genuine love, and passion was created *for* us by our loving Heavenly Father. I choose to be grateful to God for creating sexual intimacy.

Sexual intimacy with your husband is a precursor to the intimacy we will have with Christ ... our Bridegroom.

> *Thou are worthy, O lord, to receive glory and honour and power: for thou hast created all things, and for thy pleasure they are and were created.* — (Revelation 4:11, KJV)

322

JOURVOTIONAL

Super Often Sex

1. Think about your own sexual relationship with your husband. Describe the frequency of your intimacy. Do you feel it is a selfless intimacy? Why or why not?

_____

_____

_____

_____

_____

_____

_____

2. Read John 8:31-32 again. What does this phrase mean to you, "you will know the truth, and the truth will set you free," in regards to how you view sexual intimacy with your husband?

_____

_____

_____

_____

_____

3. Write out a final prayer to God. He wants you to know the truth about sexual intimacy. He wants this truth to set you free sexually. What is your prayer to your Heavenly Father regarding the truth of sexual intimacy?

_____

_____

_____

_____

_____

_____

_____

_____

_____

S.O.S.

AFTERWORD

Ray and I have been speakers for the FamilyLife "Weekend to Remember" Marriage Get-aways for over 15 years now. There is one statement said in this weekend conference that rings true for me every time I hear it: "Your marriage is not played out on a romantic balcony but on a spiritual battlefield." We must know that the attack on our sexual intimacy is Satan's way of waging war against our most precious and intimate possession. We are more than conquerors in Christ but we must continue to *fight, FIGHT, **FIGHT**!* When we are tired and cannot see progress or hope, we have to remember to arm ourselves with people who can "hold up our arms" when the battle is too overwhelming.

In 1 John 2:1, we are reminded: "My little children, I am writing these things to you so that you may not sin. But if anyone does sin, we have an advocate with the Father, Jesus Christ the righteous." Remember that when you are too tired, Christ is your advocate and will defend you until the very end.

You can go to almost every town and find good books. We are a country of intellectual readers. We no longer need experts to come into our homes to repair what is broken. We have books that tell us how to fix the plumbing, the electricity, and build an addition to our homes without the need of a trained specialist.

These books are excellent tools on fixing things; they will save you time and money. But one thing that all of these books cannot fix is your heart if it has been tricked and robbed of all that God has for you. That's right. No self-help book will ever help you if it does not point you back to "THE BOOK. The BIBLE, The Holy Word of God."

God calls us sheep in His Word because without His direction, we are just plain dumb. We can see our ignorance each time we find ourselves being made a fool of by Satan's vicious attacks on our intimacy. In John 10:11 we read, "I am the good shepherd. The good shepherd lays down his life for the sheep." God is the shepherd who wants to lead his sheep and has left for us, His Bible, the biggest book for dummies. It can take the dumb sheep and make them wise. All we have to do is read and apply the Word.

> *"But God chose what is foolish in the world to shame the wise; God chose what is weak in the world to shame the strong; God chose what is low and despised in the world, even things that are not, to bring to nothing things that are, so that no human being might boast in the presence of God. His is the source of your life in Christ Jesus, whom God made our wisdom and our righteousness and sanctification and redemption. Therefore, as it is written, "Let the one who boasts, boast in the Lord"* —(1 Corinthians 1:27-31).

Boast in what God can and will do in your intimacy. God has healed the sick, made the leper's spots clean, and raised the dead. He wants to make you wise regarding your intimacy with your husband. He can heal you because He wants you to show off to the world what He has the power to do.

God created sexual intimacy for our pleasure. He desires you to have this intimate relationship with your husband and He desires this relationship to be sinless. You must remember to fight, read, meditate, and memorize the Word of God. This will prepare your heart to be fertile ground.

When the Holy Spirit begins the process of growing your desire for intimacy with your husband, He will find a heart that is prepared for transformation. You will no longer be a woman who is sick of sex, but one who is sexually (and spiritually) satisfied, openly sharing the redeeming power of God in your marriage every opportunity you get.

We cannot, however, think that all of this is done without the enemy wanting to douse this newly lit flame. The enemy of Christian marriages has many bound in the area of sexual intimacy. We need freedom.

Satan is wreaking havoc on our marriages and our intimacy. He is holding onto you with every trick in him. But we must dispel his lies with the truth. Some of us need to write out scriptures that speak truth to us and walk around with them pasted on the backs of our hands.

We must return to the days where we memorize scripture. Memorize scripture, and you have truth, instantaneously, for every life situation. Memorizing the Word is abiding in the Word. The Bible tells us to "believe on the Lord Jesus Christ and you shall be saved" (Acts 16:31). Just as you have to believe on the Lord for salvation, you must believe God's Word for freedom from bondage. Belief is deep. If you believe that something is true, you live like this truth is real, whether you have seen it with your own eyes or not.

Want a tattoo? Tattoo an entire passage of scripture or key verses that call you to remember the truth! The

Lord will prepare your heart and you will hear Him and obey. Just humble yourself before Him.

> O Lord, you hear the desire of the afflicted; you will strengthen their heart; you will incline your ear to do justice to the fatherless and the oppressed, so that man who is of the earth may strike terror no more.
> — (Psalm 10:17-18)

Who is it that walks blamelessly, does what is right, and speaks truth in his heart? Don't we all want to have someone in our lives like that? You can be that blameless, righteous speaker of truth. God will change your heart when it is prepared to receive what God has for it.

> He who walks blamelessly and does what is right and speaks truth in his heart.
> — (Psalm 15:2)

Ask God to search your heart and remove all the evil that is there. Then ask Him to lead you in His everlasting way.

> Search me, O God, and know my heart: try me and know my thoughts: And see if there

be any wicked way in me, and lead me in the
way everlasting. — Psalm 139:23-24

When God changes your heart, it will be reflected on your face. The enemy of your marriage would love for you to continue to have sorrow of heart in this intimate sexual relationship knowing that if your spirit is crushed then you will respond to life being crushed. When your spirit is crushed in any area, it is also reflected on your face.

A glad heart makes a cheerful face, but by
sorrow of heart the spirit is crushed.
— (Proverbs 15:13)

What is abundant in your heart? If your heart is filled to abundance with good, you will bring forth good. If you want a marriage that brings God glory and gives you pleasure, then you must begin to prepare your heart for transformation. God wants fertile ground where He can do a good work.

For out of the abundance of the heart the
mouth speaks. A good man out of the treas-
ure of the heart brings forth good.
— (Matthew 12:34-35)

APPENDIX I

SCRIPTURES ON SEX

Biblical Phrases for Sex

"Knew" — Genesis 4:1, 4:17, 4:25, 19:8, 24:16; Numbers 31:17-18; Judges 2:11-12

"Went into" — Genesis 16:4

"Gave to your embrace" — Genesis 16:5

"Rejoice in the wife of your youth" — Proverbs 5:18-19

Times to Withhold/Wait for Sex

When both agree for a time of prayer/fasting — 1 Corinthians 7:5

Forbidden Sex

With someone else's wife — Leviticus 18:20

With the same sex — Romans 1:24, 26-27.

New Testament Punishments for Sexual Immorality

Will not inherit the kingdom of God — 1 Corinthians 6:9-10

Why Flee Sexual Immorality — 1 Corinthians 6:13-20

Why Sex in Marriage — 1 Corinthians 7:1-4

APPENDIX II

RECOMMENDED INTIMACY RESOURCES

1. *Intimate Issues*, Linda Dillow/Lorraine Pintus, 1999, Waterbrook press

2. *Intimate Allies*, Dan Allender/Tremper Longman III, 1995,

3. *Intended for Pleasure*, Ed Wheat and Gaye Wheat, 1977, Revell Books

4. *Sheet Music*, Kevin Leman, 2003, Tyndale House Publishers

APPENDIX III

SONG OF SOLOMON
1:2-15

The Song of Solomon is a moving love story between a young country girl and King Solomon. In delicate poetry, the lovers express intense passion and deep longing for each other. The young girl compares her love for her husband to the anticipation of a frantic search, while Solomon likens his bride's beauty to picturesque gardens and delicious fruit.

Yet even in this eloquent expression of the passion between a bride and bridegroom, there is an exhortation to remain sexually pure before marriage (2:7). In this way, the book celebrates human sexuality within the context of marriage.[2]

2   *Let him kiss me with the kisses of his mouth—*
     for your love is more delightful than wine.

[2] Radmacher, E. D., Allen, R. B., & House, H. W. *The Nelson Study Bible: New King James Version* (Nashville: Thomas Nelson Publishers, 1997), Song of Solomon 1:1

3   *Pleasing is the fragrance of your perfumes;*
      your name is like perfume poured out.
      No wonder the maidens love you!

4   *Take me away with you—let us hurry!*
      Let the king bring me into his chambers.

Friends
      We rejoice and delight in you;
      we will praise your love more than wine.

Beloved
      How right they are to adore you!

5   *Dark am I, yet lovely,*
      O daughters of Jerusalem,
      dark like the tents of Kedar,
      like the tent curtains of Solomon.

6   *Do not stare at me because I am dark,*
      because I am darkened by the sun.
      My mother's sons were angry with me
      and made me take care of the vineyards;
      my own vineyard I have neglected.

7   *Tell me, you whom I love, where you graze your flock*
      and where you rest your sheep at midday.
      Why should I be like a veiled woman
      beside the flocks of your friends?

Friends

8   *If you do not know, most beautiful of women,*
      follow the tracks of the sheep
      and graze your young goats

by the tents of the shepherds.

Lover

9   *I liken you, my darling, to a mare*
    harnessed to one of the chariots of Pharaoh.

10 *Your cheeks are beautiful with earrings,*
    your neck with strings of jewels.

11 *We will make you earrings of gold,*
    studded with silver.

Beloved

12 *While the king was at his table,*
    my perfume spread its fragrance.

13 *My lover is to me a sachet of myrrh*
    resting between my breasts.

14 *My lover is to me a cluster of henna blossoms*
    from the vineyards of En Gedi.

Lover

15 *How beautiful you are, my darling!*
    Oh, how beautiful!
    Your eyes are doves.

Photo by evantardy.com

www.robynmckelvy.com